THIS BOOK BELONGS TO

Roselyn Benon

ROYAL PARAMOURS

Other books by Dulcie M. Ashdown
Queen Victoria's Mother
Queen Victoria's Family

ROYAL
PARAMOURS

Dulcie M. Ashdown

DORSET PRESS
New York

First published by Robert Hale Limited, 1979

This edition published by Dorset Press,
a division of Marboro Books Corporation,
by arrangement with
Robert Hale Limited.

1986 Dorset Press.

ISBN 0-88029-093-5
(Formerly ISBN 0-7091-7151-X)

Printed in the United States of America

M 9 8 7 6 5 4 3

Contents

Acknowledgements

The quotations from manuscripts at Blenheim have been granted by kind permission of His Grace the Duke of Marlborough.

Use of other quotations in copyright has been authorised by the following publishers:

W. H. Allen & Co. Ltd. *The love letters of Henry VIII*, ed. H. Savage (Allen Wingate, 1949).

Associated Book Publishers Ltd. *Materials for a history of the reign of George II*, ed. R. Sedgwick, three volumes (Eyre & Spottiswoode Ltd., 1931).

Basil Blackwell. *The prose works of Jonathan Swift*, ed. H. Davis (1953).

Cassell & Co. Ltd. *The Correspondence of George, Prince of Wales, 1770–1812*, ed. A. Aspinall (1963–71).

Peter Davies Ltd. G. Renier, *William of Orange* (1932).

Evans Brothers Ltd. *Dearest Mama*, ed. R. Fulford (1968).

George G. Harrap & Co. Ltd. W. S. Churchill, *Marlborough: his life and times* (1947).

William Heinemann Ltd. C. H. Hartmann, *The King my brother* (1954).

Oxford University Press. D. Mancini, *The usurpation of Richard III*, trs. C. A. J. Armstrong, second edition (Clarendon Press, 1969); H. Walpole, *Reminiscences*, ed. E. Paget Toynbee (Clarendon Press, 1924); Thomas Nelson & Sons Ltd. *Vita Edwardi Secundi*, ed. N. Denholm Young (1957).

Penguin Books Ltd. G. Chaucer, *The Canterbury Tales*, trs. N. Coghill (1960).

The Roxburghe Club. James II, *Papers of devotion*, ed. G. Davies (1925).

Sidgwick & Jackson. M. Gillen, *The Prince and his lady* (1970).

Yale University Press Ltd. T. More, *The history of King Richard III*, ed. R. S. Sylvester (complete works, 1963).

Illustrations

PICTURE CREDITS

By gracious permission of H.M. the Queen (photograph by A. C. Cooper Ltd.), No 21; the British Museum, 1 and 18; the Provost and Fellows of Eton College (photograph by courtesy of the Courtauld Institute of Art), 2; from the collection of the late Denys Eyre Bower of Chiddingstone Castle, near Edenbridge, Kent, 10; the administrator, Blenheim Palace (photographs by Jeremy Whitaker), 11 and 14; from the collection of the Earl of Jersey, 12; his Grace the Duke of Atholl and the National Galleries of Scotland (photograph by Tom Scott), 15; from the Raymond Mander and Joe Mitchenson Theatre Collection, 22; the National Portrait Gallery, 3, 4, 5, 6, 7, 8, 9, 13 and 17; other pictures from the Radio Times Hulton Picture Library.

Introduction

The permissive society is no twentieth-century invention: for hundreds of years sexual promiscuity has been, if not always the norm, at least as widespread as it is today; only our frankness on the subject is new.

In fact, on several counts modern sexual morality is 'cleaner' than that of the past, comparing favourably even with that of the supposedly respectable era of the Victorians. In late nineteenth-century London, one house in six was a brothel; today the statistic has been estimated at nearer one in sixteen thousand—and the infamous child prostitution has been eradicated. In country areas and town slums the illegitimacy rate, in the years after birth-registration was initiated, was of startling proportions—effective modern birth-control may have encouraged promiscuity but it has gone a long way towards minimising the ill-effects of illegitimate births: once, a girl who had 'got into trouble' had no recourse but prostitution to provide for herself and her child.

Britain's upper classes have never been noted for their moral leadership of the nation: in past centuries a nobleman without a mistress was a rarity; a king without a harem almost a freak.

Modern royal marriages are made for love—easier to achieve since today's princes and princesses are not confined to the narrow circle of their own caste in seeking life-partners. Until this century, however, the arranged marriage was the norm, with parental interests and international politics usually dictating the selection of a royal bride or groom. With loveless marriages and generally accepted sexual latitude, it was no wonder that kings and princes felt free to fornicate and commit adultery with impunity.

A historian becomes unshockable. Moral judgement of the personal life of a monarch is irrelevant to any assessment of that monarch's reign, except when royal sexuality interferes with royal government. A good king was one who did not over-tax his subjects or drive them into the miseries of war for his personal gain; fidelity to his wife was rarely relevant to such virtue.

Today, just as no British monarch would claim the divine right to rule according to personal whim, none would place himself above his subjects' moral standards. Indeed, in recent years the nation has come to expect moral as well as social leadership from the royal family. A Victorian lady, regaled with the antics of the Egyptian Queen Cleopatra on stage, is said to have remarked, "So unlike the home life of our own dear Queen!": just so might one compare the domestic bliss of modern Windsor and Buckingham Palace with the escapades in castles and palaces of the past.

And yet, who can deny the fascination of a royal love-story? The bulk of modern fiction deals with irregular love-relationships of one sort and another: the course of true love, blessed by church and convention, makes dull reading. And, in the lives of the kings and queens of the past, truth is more flamboyant than fiction could ever be. Here are stories which make 'paperback passion' look tame in contrast. They may not edify, but they cannot fail to amuse.

ROYAL PARAMOURS

I

The Maiden, Friend of the Lord King

1066: the one date in English history that everyone knows. Recent historians have sought to demonstrate that that date was by no means as significant as is generally thought: they have denied the importance of the Norman Conquest in terms of government, economics and social life, and of the replacement of a Saxon by a Norman on England's throne. But it is hard to undo the work of centuries: 1066 retains its power.

In fact, in a history of royal paramours, 1066 is a valid starting-point, for the Norman usurper of the English throne, William the Conqueror, was himself a bastard.

He was the son of Duke Robert of Normandy and Herleve (or Arlette) of Falaise. There is no hint in any of the chronicles or legends that Herleve was a professional prostitute: she was merely one of the peasants over whom the Duke might exercise his *droit de seigneur*, apparently first seen and admired by Robert while she was in alluring disarray washing her clothes at the river. Herleve's father, Fulbert, was a tanner and, contemporary sources suggest, a brewer and part-time undertaker, and she seems to have inherited his flair for private enterprise, for she exploited her opportunity to the full. Herleve was no 'one night stand', enjoyed and forgotten, but held the Duke's interest long enough to bear him two children, William and Adelaide, and took her reward in the form of marriage to Herluin, Vicomte de Conteville—a brilliant match for a peasant-girl, which may be a tribute to her charms and attractions but more probably to Herluin's obedience to his overlord, eager to make provision for a valued mistress.

The Duke of Normandy had no legitimate children and, at his death in 1035, designated William as his heir. Inevitably, the nobles related to the Norman dukes balked at accepting Robert's bastard (only some seven years old) as his successor, and for ten years Normandy was troubled by civil war between the young Duke William's enemies and his supporters. Then, in 1047, his ally the King of France defeated the rebels at the battle of Val-ès-dunes, and though William had always to be wary of his vassals' notions of independence, he was thereafter in control of his duchy. And from Normandy, in 1066, he came to England, to wrest the crown from Harold. The peasant-girl's son became a king.

Not surprisingly, William himself ensured that he had legitimate sons in plenty to carry on the Norman line, but, at the same time, he is not known to have had any children born out of wedlock. Modern psychologists would certainly find good reasons for this in the circumstances of his own birth: contemporaries merely praised his continence.

Marital fidelity was by no means common among kings and aristocrats of the Middle Ages. For the most part, they made loveless marriages and looked elsewhere for affection and sexual stimulation.

Usually a royal marriage was arranged when bride and groom were in their early teens—arranged by their fathers with an eye to a good dowry, a political alliance or some other benefit to themselves as well as to their children. From birth, a princess could expect to leave home and family to go to a bridegroom in a far country, a man she might never have seen before she faced him at the altar. Love sometimes came after marriage, but not invariably. Many a woman knew that her husband regarded her as a mere producer of children, a *châtelaine* and ornament, though, at the same time, where there was no love between husband and wife, the wife need feel no deep pain when her husband took a mistress, be it for love or lust: her pride might be hurt; she might resent his generosity to another woman and her children; but she could not, as a modern wife would, charge her husband with breaking vows of eternal love.

On the other hand, women had no such latitude in sexual relationships as men enjoyed. An unmarried woman of any status was kept in seclusion, among her family and her mother's female servants, until the time came for her to marry: a girl who could not bring her maidenhead to her wedding was ruined for life, unlikely to find a husband, for no man would ever trust her not to dishonour him once her own honour had been called in doubt. Nor could a wife expect the latitude of extra-marital *affaires* which her husband claimed. Pride apart, no great lord would wish to see his lands, castles and wealth inherited by another man's son passed off as his own. Where men took their own pleasures carelessly, they were always vigilant over their wives' fidelity—though stories of the chastity-belts worn by the stay-at-home wives of Crusaders have been exaggerated.

Some royal marriages of the three centuries after the Conquest were models of harmony and affection: those of King Stephen and Matilda of Boulogne, of Edward I and Eleanor of Castile, for example. To this day one may see the 'Eleanor crosses' raised by a grief-stricken Edward I on the resting-places of his wife's coffin on its journey from Grantham, where she died in 1290, to Charing Cross, the last overnight stop before her burial at Westminster: an eloquent testimony to married love.

The marriage of Henry II and Eleanor of Aquitaine was, indeed, reputed to be the result of a grand passion, as well as of Henry's lust for Eleanor's duchy of Aquitaine. Perhaps such intensity of feeling explains the Queen's fierce, bitter jealousy of her husband's mistresses, and the classic love-hate relationship which developed between Henry and Eleanor in later life.

Sexual morality in the Middle Ages veered between extremes: at one pole, there was the chastity of thousands of monks and nuns; at the other such reputations as those of Henry I of England, the father of more than twenty bastards, and of the Emperor Frederick Barbarossa, a German who rivalled Henry in fabled virility. Fornication and adultery were condemned by the Church, but it would be a brave priest who would not give absolution to a king—even when he knew perfectly well that that king would not heed the injunction to "go and sin no more".

Where an overlord had the power of life and death over his serfs, he would certainly have no scruples in 'having his will' of any attractive peasant-girl who caught his eye. Only when a king lusted after a woman of high rank did his sins attract attention: an outraged Breton lord, for example, charged Henry II with seducing his daughter while she was in his custody as a hostage; King John was widely reviled by his barons for raping their wives and daughters.

It is impossible to give any detailed and reliable account of the mistresses of the English kings in the first three centuries after the Conquest. There are few references to them in the kingdom's annals. What evidence there is comes mainly from the pens of disapproving monkish chroniclers, who, if they had a spite against a particular king, might make him appear a monstrous lecher to add to his other sins. Some evidence may be found in royal household accounts, though even this is not wholly reliable. There is, for instance, in the Pipe Rolls of the thirtieth year of Henry II's reign, the following entry: "For clothes and hoods and cloaks and for the trimming of two capes of samite and for the clothes of the Queen and Bellebelle, for the King's use, £55 17 shillings, by the King's writ."[1] Despite the indelicacy of ranging a queen with a whore, this entry has been read by some historians to mean that 'Bellebelle' (the very name has a boudoir ring to it) was Henry II's mistress. Just as puzzling is an entry in the Misae Rolls of King John, a grant of clothes to one Suzanne, *"domicella, amica domini regis"*, "the maiden, friend of the lord king"[2]—though evidence elsewhere confirms speculation as to her status by naming her as the mother of John's son Richard.

It is, in fact, largely by counting royal bastards that one may draw conclusions as to the promiscuity of the medieval kings. From the fact that Henry I is known to have acknowledged at least twenty illegitimate children, it may be deduced (even without the chroniclers' many reprovals) that the King was a great womaniser, that he probably had many more mistresses than those who gave birth to his known offspring: there may have been innumerable 'one-night stands' who made no lasting impression on their royal lover, who did not conceive, who remained in obscurity.

However, it is possible to know, from chronicles and charters, that among the number of Henry I's mistresses was at least one member of the conquered Saxon race, for she had the English name Edith, a noble Norman lady, Isabelle de Beaumont (sister of the Earl of Leicester and Count of Meulan, herself later the wife of the Earl of Pembroke) and a Welsh princess named Nesta.

To Nesta at least we may ascribe some attraction of beauty or charm, for a contemporary with a knowledge of the classics named her 'the Helen of Wales', and she figured in a minor tragedy which had its origins in a man's lust for her.

After her liaison with Henry I, Nesta had married one Gerald of Windsor, Constable of Pembroke, and went to live with him in her native land. It was there that she was seen and desired by Owain ap Cadwgan, a Welsh lord of Cardigan. Owain had the temerity to abduct Nesta, arousing not only Windsor's but also the King's wrath. He was forced to flee to Ireland, and it was several years before he dared return to Wales, but soon after his arrival there he made his peace with King Henry, in 1114. Gerald was not so forgiving: in 1116 he hired a gang of Flemings to murder the Welsh philanderer. Nesta, presumably, was more closely guarded after her adventure and in time may have become a staid and respectable matron: her family, indeed, became eminently respectable, with one of her sons a bishop, another a military commander in Henry II's conquest of Ireland.

If dozens of chronicles must be scanned to find even the mere names of royal mistresses, it is equally frustrating to seek evidence of their rewards in the household accounts of the medieval kings. It may be reasonable to speculate that a peasant-girl was paid for her services with a silver or copper coin, but there is not a shred of evidence for it; a royal mistress housed at Court may have received gifts of clothes, as did Bellebelle and Suzanne—but then so did most of the royal retainers, high and low. We know that Herleve of Falaise and Nesta of Wales were married off to their lovers' vassals, thereby assuring them a life of comfort and security: maybe other mistresses were similarly provided for; some may be among the many ladies who were assigned rents for royal manors for their upkeep and that of their children, listed among the more respectable women who received pensions from the king. But so often such evidence is ambiguous. There is an instance of King John's releasing William de Fortibus, Count of Aumâle, from his debts to the Crown: William's mother, the widowed Countess Hawisa, is known to have been one of John's mistresses, which may account for his generosity to the family; but then again, it might have been a reward for William's loyalty or service.

Whatever the kings' generosity to their mistresses, there is firm evidence that many accepted the responsibilities of paternity, providing for their illegitimate children: at the same time, by raising them to noble rank and marrying them into the nobility, the royal fathers could use their bastards as they did their legitimate offspring, to strengthen their own power. Henry I gave two of his many daughters in marriage to the Counts of Perche and Brittany, ensuring support from these men in his Continental territories; one of King John's daughters, Joan, was married in 1204 to Llewellyn the Great, Prince of Gwynedd in Wales, to give the King an ally against the pretensions of another Welsh prince. Joan served her father well on her own account also: when John and Llewellyn were in arms against each other in 1211, she went to mediate between them and gained peace—though at terms which crushed the Welsh. A year later, when John was planning a descent into Wales to put down rebellion, Joan was sent to warn him that if he did so, he would be a marked man, for her husband's friends planned to kidnap him. (Later the Princess spoiled this excellent record: she committed adultery with William de Braose, lord of Abergavenny; Llewellyn hanged the lover and imprisoned his wife.) The most splendid marriage of all was that of another of Henry I's daughters, Sybil, with Alexander I, King of Scotland: no real princess could expect a better match.

As to the sons of royal mistresses, some of them were to be numbered among the richest and most powerful royal vassals. Robert of Caen, allegedly the eldest of Henry I's bastards, was given many English manors, the hand in marriage of Mabel fitzHamon, heiress of Glamorgan, and, in 1122, the earldom of Gloucester, while his brother Reginald became Earl of Cornwall. Of Henry II's illegitimate sons, William Longsword was created Earl of Salisbury, and Geoffrey (son of a low-bred Anglo-Saxon prostitute named Ykenai—one of the few professionals known to be a royal mistress, who reputedly "scorned no filthiness" in relations with her clients) became Bishop of Lincoln in his father's lifetime and Archbishop of York in the reign of his half-brother Richard I, despite the fact that bastards were in theory barred from high office in the Church.

It is not too outrageous, surely, to suggest that when a king was generous to a son or daughter, he had some abiding affection for the mother? But again, where is the evidence? Who was Sybil Corbet, the mother of Robert of Caen, that her son won such favours from Henry I? What were Ykenai's charms that Henry II should so elevate her son? Where is there any evidence as to how long any royal mistress shared a king's bed, let alone whether or not he ever loved her?

Certainly there must have been some degree of family feeling between fathers and children, brothers and sisters. When the famous White Ship went down in 1120, on a crossing from

Normandy, Henry I's legitimate son William risked his life to go to the assistance of one of his half-sisters, the Countess of Perche: both were drowned. Robert, Earl of Gloucester, firmly championed the cause of his legitimate half-sister Matilda when she sought to take the crown, and for years (from 1135 until his death in 1147) fought battle after battle in her name against their cousin Stephen, the usurper. Robert, brave and intelligent, a respected leader of men, cultured beyond the norm of contemporary nobles, might have been a great king himself, and it is a tribute to his loyalty that he never used his wide following to challenge for the throne on his own account. It would have been a feasible pretension. Two generations later, William Longsword's fraternal feeling for King John went so far as to keep him loyal when so many of his fellow-barons were in revolt; he deserted John briefly in 1215 but, when the King was hardest pressed by his barons (self-confident after forcing John to concede the terms of Magna Carta) and by the incursions of the French, he returned to his allegiance.

Henry II bitterly regretted the inferiority of his true-born sons to his bastards. When the princes rebelled against him in 1173–4 (abetted by their mother, Eleanor of Aquitaine), it was the illegitimate Geoffrey who rode against them in his father's army—to be rewarded by Henry's remark, "You alone have proved yourself my lawful and true son; my other sons are really the bastards!"[3] And again, when the princes were in revolt in 1189, towards the end of Henry II's life, Geoffrey was with him; he was the only one of the King's sons to attend him on his death-bed.

However, though it seems that Geoffrey had some idea of claiming the throne after Henry's death, he never had the opportunity. His half-brother Richard I made him take his final vows as a priest immediately: Geoffrey became Archbishop of York, but now he could look no higher.

Of course, there were exceptions to the general rule of family loyalty rendered by the children of medieval kings. The most notable is the case of Juliana, one of Henry I's daughters, who even tried to kill her father (according to one, admittedly dubious, source). She was the wife of Eustace, Count of Breteuil in Normandy, one of her father's vassals, but if the King had married her to the Count to buy his loyalty, he was to be disappointed. Eustace's later demand for a certain fortress aroused his father-in-law's suspicions that he was planning rebellion, and though Henry dared not refuse Eustace in case this further alienated him, he yielded the stronghold only on condition that the Count surrender to him his young daughters (the King's own grandchildren) as hostages, as an act of good faith. In exchange, Eustace was given custody of the young son of Harenc, the then governor of the castle.

The Count of Breteuil betrayed his trust: he barbarously blinded the child in his care. Equally incomprehensible to modern sensibilities, King Henry advised Harenc to take revenge by treating Eustace's daughters in the same manner. He also marched up to the castle and laid siege to it, preparing his forces for attack.

Countess Juliana, in command of the castle in her husband's absence, was not at first prepared to yield to her father. In fact, she appeared on the battlements and fired an arrow at King Henry's heart—but she missed. Soon afterwards, realising that resistance was useless, she surrendered, but the King had already torn down the drawbridge, and the only way she could leave the castle was by having her people lower her down the walls on a rope, into the moat. It was winter-time, and she had to wade through icy water to reach the bank, her father's men taunting her at each step.

It is a dreadful story, though one not well substantiated. In fact, Henry I was notoriously cruel to his enemies when he had them in his grasp; but on the other hand, he was notably indulgent to his children. So the story of Juliana de Breteuil might, or might not, be true.

Besides the problems of lack of evidence, dubious evidence, one story contradicting another, there is that of romantic legend, where an original fact—or misconception—was embroidered on by later story-tellers. The tales that grew up around the romance of Henry II and 'the fair Rosamund' are innumerable, enlarged upon by the fantasies of later poets and dramatists who took this royal mistress as their heroine.

Henry had married, at the age of nineteen, the internationally famed beauty and rich heiress Eleanor, Duchess of Aquitaine. She was some years his senior, the divorced wife of King Louis VII of France, and had, in fact, an amatory record of her own (it was alleged that she had bestowed generous favours on her own uncle, Raimond of Poitou, when she and King Louis had been in the sultry and sensual East on crusade). For some years Eleanor enthralled her second husband, but she was a wilful and contentious woman, not of the usual run of complaisant and dutiful queens, and in the end Henry II turned for solace elsewhere.

One of his mistresses was Rosamund, daughter of Walter de Clifford, a royal vassal. How she and Henry met, how he laid siege to her virtue, why he so honoured her that her fame grew, remains unknown. Certainly from about 1166 chroniclers were referring to her deprecatingly, not as the 'rose of the world' as the Latin of her name suggested, but as *"rosa-immundi"*, "the rose of unchastity".

Here legend and fable step in. One story, of medieval origin, tells how the jealous Queen Eleanor suddenly descended on her rival at the palace of Woodstock: the girl took fright and ran into the maze in the grounds, but an unwinding skein of embroidery silk in her pocket left a trail for the Queen to follow, and at length she came upon Rosamund at the centre of the labyrinth. There, Eleanor offered her a choice of the means of death, poison or a dagger, and so 'the fair Rosamund' was forced to die. Many are the variations on this theme in the popular literature of the Middle Ages.

In fact, when Rosamund died, in 1176, Queen Eleanor was nowhere near her. The Queen had wreaked her revenge on her husband in a far more potent way than by killing his mistress: she had raised Poitou in revolt against Henry—and for her machinations had been imprisoned.

Many chroniclers agree that Rosamund died at the convent of Godstow, near Woodstock, asserting that she had long since retired there to do penance for her sins. So sincere was her penitence that the nuns came to revere and love her, and they raised her tomb at the very foot of their chapel's altar, incising upon it the inscription *"Hic jacet in tumba Rosamundi non Rosamunda; non redolet sed olet quae redolere solet"*: "Here lieth in tomb the rose of the world, not a clean rose; it smelleth not sweet but it stinketh that was wont to smell full sweet."[4]

In 1191 a visitation by St Hugh, Bishop of Lincoln, saw the destruction of the tomb. The Bishop was shocked by the honour done to the corpse of the royal mistress and ordered its removal to the nuns' private cemetery.

But again, can this story be relied upon for truth? Similar

tales were told of other royal mistresses and their tombs, most
notably of the famous Agnes Sorel, mistress of King Charles
VIII of France.

Queen Eleanor's jealousy of Rosamund, which drove her to
conspire against Henry II, is the only certain case in these years
of a royal mistress's affecting national affairs to any real extent—
though when Eleanor's son John raped the wives and daughters
of his nobles some years later, his conduct did contribute to
their estrangement from him.

However, it is possible that Henry II's seduction of a French
princess (some years after Rosamund's death) may have had
some bearing on his ever-worsening relations with France and
with his legitimate sons—though that cannot be conclusively
asserted. Henry was intermittently at war with France throughout his reign for several reasons, and his sons had many other
grievances beyond the fact that their father withheld the
French princess Alice (or Aloysia or Adelaide, as chroniclers
name her variously) from Prince Richard, to whom she had
been betrothed.

Alice had come into the Plantagenet family in 1161, given
by her brother the French King Philippe II Augustus as a
pledge of the Anglo-French peace arranged at Fréteval. But her
wedding with Henry's son never took place. Alice was put into
the English King's keeping, but he never took steps to turn the
betrothal into marriage. Possibly, the reason given by most
chroniclers, that Alice's dowry was never handed over, is sufficient to explain the default, but a contemporary claimed that
Henry seduced his prospective daughter-in-law, keeping her for
himself when he should have given her to his son.

Certainly, Alice was used for years as a bargaining-counter
between Henry and Philippe, Henry and his sons, so the King
must have had little regard for her feelings. Time and again the
French king demanded that his sister be married forthwith;
time and again Henry agreed, only to slip out of the promise
later. The fiancé, Richard, made frequent demands for his
bride—but he may have been looking more to her dowry than
to her person. Sentimental Victorian historians liked to see him
as fighting to win Alice during his father's reign, but then they
have to shift stance, seeing that he repudiated her when he
became king and married another princess (Alice was then sent
home and soon afterwards married a French knight, so her

unhappy adolescence may have been compensated for by a stable life in later years).

Once again, even where contemporary accounts are quite full, as in the case of Princess Alice, it is impossible to gauge motive and feeling with any degree of certainty. Women were of so little account in the early Middle Ages, even royal ladies, that few chroniclers troubled to mention them, and when they did, they did not always bother to record their names correctly, let alone tell their life-stories in a reliable and detailed manner.

Fortunately, from the fourteenth century onwards, the picture becomes increasingly clearer. The homosexual partners of King Edward II played a leading role in the politics of his reign and attracted a good deal of attention from contemporary chroniclers, and the royal mistresses of the following century had such strong personalities that they made their mark in the history of their lovers' reigns.

2

That Vain Light-headed Earl

England had three homosexual kings in the Middle Ages:
William II, Richard I (though there the evidence is slight) and
Edward II, whose propensities were a considerable factor in the
build-up to the rebellion which ended his reign.

William II, the son of William the Conqueror, was a red-
haired or ruddy-complexioned man, from which he became
known as 'Rufus'. No one, it seems, had a good word for him
during his reign, apart from the choice band of minions who
constituted his Court: clerics preached against them from the
pulpit, monks fulminated against them in their chronicles of the
era. One of these, William of Malmesbury, recorded that:

Then was there flowing hair and extravagant dress [for men],
and then was invented the fashion of shoes with curved points,
then the model for young men was to rival women in delicacy of
person, to mince their gait, to walk with loose gesture, and half
naked. Enervated and effeminate, they unwillingly remained what
nature had made them, the assailer of others' chastity, prodigal
of their own. Troops of pathics and droves of whores followed the
Court.[1]

There is less evidence for the tastes of Richard I: he was more
than once charged by the clergy to leave off "unnatural vices"
and to live with his Spanish wife, who in the end left him, but
he was a generally popular king, much praised by contemporary
chroniclers, who could forgive much in view of Richard's valiant
adventures in the Holy Land.

For Edward II, however, much detail is available, an indication of contemporaries' horror of his habits, or, more correctly,
of their political consequences.

The first indications of his homosexuality appear in the lifetime of his father, the uxorious Edward I, who was furious
when the Prince asked permission to bestow one of his own
titles, that of Count of Ponthieu, on his friend Piers Gaveston,

a young Gascon squire of his household. The King was incensed at the idea of his son, who had never won any land in war, freely bestowing a county on a man who by no means merited such an honour: Gaveston was banished from England, but accompanied to the port of Dover by the now infatuated Prince.

However, this incident occurred in the spring of 1307, and on 7 July 1307 King Edward I died: the first act of the new King was to recall Piers Gaveston, whom he created Earl of Cornwall and whom he now planned to marry to his own niece, Margaret de Clare, who was sister and co-heiress of one of the greatest English nobles, the Earl of Gloucester. After spending Christmas with his friend, Edward appointed him Keeper of the Realm (an office usually reserved for elderly counsellors of proven wisdom and integrity), when he left for France, to marry the daughter of the French king.

The young King's attachment to Gaveston may not, until this time, have appeared overly heinous. Homosexuality was apparently widespread among the aristocrats of the Middle Ages, not unusual in the male-orientated military caste, though frequently denounced by the clergy (ironically, for medieval monks were among the worst offenders). It seems, however, that many of those who practised sodomy were in fact bisexual, capable of fathering children (as was Edward II himself): presumably, at least among the aristocracy, heterosexual relations were regarded by those with homosexual preferences as a duty imposed by their rank, to ensure the continuance in their line of great titles and estates. Thus, it was not Edward's homosexuality itself which so offended his subjects but his increasing dependence on his lover Gaveston.

At first many may have regarded the King's propensities as an adolescent, passing phase. As one of the characters in the play on Edward II's life, by the Tudor playwright Christopher Marlowe, was to express it,

> The mightiest kings have had their minions:
> Great Alexander loved Ephestion.
> The conquering Hercules for Itis wept,
>   And for Patroclus stern Achilles;
> And not kings only but the wisest men:
> The Roman Tully loved Octavius,
>   Grave Socrates, wild Alcibiades.
> Then let his Grace, whose youth is flexible

And promiseth as much as we can wish,
Freely enjoy that vain light-headed earl,
For riper years will wean him from such toys.[2]

However, Edward did not outgrow his love for Gaveston, and his early proof of that love, honouring him with titles and power, was soon followed with other demonstrations of his dependence on his lover, which angered his rightful counsellors, the higher nobility and the bishops. And Gaveston himself did nothing to assuage their jealousy and indignation but intensified their grievances by treating the barons with contempt.

Only nine months after Edward's accession, a party of lords in Parliament demanded Gaveston's banishment. Once again, Edward himself escorted his friend to the port of embarkation, fawning on him openly to the last moment.

At this point, the King showed the first glimmers of political acumen: he made an effort to appease his lords on one hand, and on the other to split the opposition party. By 1309 he was strong enough to have Gaveston recalled. Unfortunately, the Earl had learned no lesson from past events but was as conceited and overbearing as ever. His enemies re-united and within only a few months Edward and Gaveston were parted again, and the King was left to face a crisis in government, with demands for redress of grievance forced on him by the peers who were soon calling themselves the 'Lords Ordainers'. Edward offered to yield to them any of the reforms for which they pressed on the one condition that Gaveston be left unharmed: the Ordainers refused.

When the Ordinances were proclaimed in London in September 1311, one of their clauses provided for Gaveston's banishment. Again he left, but within weeks it was rumoured that he had returned secretly and was to be found hiding in the royal apartments. At Christmas he appeared at the King's side.

The opening of the year 1312 saw the two men journeying into Scotland, in the hope of persuading King Robert Bruce to give Gaveston sanctuary. But they were to be disappointed and, when they attempted to return south, found themselves threatened by armies led against them by the now exasperated barons. Edward left Gaveston, apparently intending to face them with an army, and the Earl took refuge in Scarborough Castle. But after a fortnight, when the King and his reinforcements had not appeared, Gaveston was forced to come to terms with the besieging army: he was guaranteed safe conduct, on condition that he present himself at the next Parliament to account for his crimes. Unfortunately for Gaveston, there were among his captors lords who did not consider themselves bound in honour to keep their word to such a man. On the way south, while the cavalcade rested at Deddington on 9 June, the Earl of Warwick took possession of the prisoner, swept him off to his own citadel and, on 19 June, had him beheaded.

Understandably, King Edward II was overcome with grief, and from that moment planned revenge, though at the time he was in no position to do anything but submit to the barons.

In fact, it might even now have been possible for Edward to salvage his dignity, to make amends to his lords and to begin afresh on the task of ruling England. Indeed it did seem that he was willing to make an effort in improving relations with his wife, who had been ignored and slighted during the reign of Gaveston. Only five months after the death of the royal favourite, Queen Isabelle gave birth to her first child, the future King Edward III, and for some time afterwards the royal couple appeared to cohabit in all amity. In October 1313 the King and his barons made their peace, formally and decisively, and the future promised well.

Then, in 1314, things began to go wrong again. Edward's campaign against the Scots proved disastrous, most notably with his humiliating defeat at the Battle of Bannockburn. In his resulting weakness, he was forced to capitulate to the Ordainers, now under the leadership of his cousin Thomas, Earl of Lancaster (formerly one of the leading enemies of Gaveston and a prime mover in the events of 1312). In the months that followed, Lancaster took complete control of the royal government.

If a graph were to be drawn of the fortunes of King Edward II, the line for the years 1314–21 would ascend gradually, dip in 1321, then rise steeply in 1322. First, using guile, and the loyalty of such as the Earl of Pembroke, who sought a middle way in politics, the King re-established himself as a force in government, putting his friends in key positions with power sufficient to block Lancaster's measures for reform. In 1317 the King and the Earl stood on the brink of civil war, but it was averted, and it was only in 1321 that a new crisis threatened.

A major factor in the situation was the King's new love. For some years he had been distinguishing one Hugh Despencer with favours and rewards, giving him an heiress bride and supporting his territorial ambitions in the Welsh Marches. In 1321 Lancaster struck at Despencer, arraigning him (and his father, of the same name) in Parliament at Westminster that July: history repeated itself with the sentence of banishment inflicted on the royal favourite. But this obvious repetition of old defeats was too much for Edward, who mounted an attack on Lancaster's adherents among the Marcher Lords, defeated them in battle and then turned on the Earl himself. At Borough-bridge, near York, Lancaster's forces were routed, himself captured. The Earl was tried at Pontefract and, convicted of treason, beheaded on 22 March 1322.

So Edward had yet another chance to redeem himself, and for the first time since his accession a chance to rule without deference to an opposition party. And, indeed, for some time, he seemed to be set fair for a quiet, successful reign, notably merciful to his enemies, considerate in the granting of just reforms, not even overly generous to his favourite.

In fact, it cannot be certainly claimed that Despencer was the King's homosexual partner, for contemporary chroniclers were less specific in their charges against him than they had been against Gaveston. Nevertheless, there are indications that they were lovers, not the least of which is the fact that Queen Isabelle so distinctly loathed the man who now ousted her from her husband's affections.

Isabelle had suffered a good deal since she had arrived in England as a twelve-year-old bride. Even at her wedding feast, Edward had so openly caressed Gaveston that her uncles had retired in disgust; in the years that followed, she had seen the favourite decked in the jewels which she had brought in her dowry and awarded estates which should have fallen to the share of the royal consort; in 1314, when Edward and Gaveston had made a hurried flight from Newcastle as the Ordainers' forces approached, the Queen, three months pregnant, had been left behind to fend for herself. The years 1312–21 were the happiest in her married life, with Gaveston dead and Despencer not yet usurping her role, and she bore her husband four children in those years. But when Despencer took command in 1322, she was once again relegated to a second place, and from this time she may have been planning the measures which she would one day set in train to take her revenge. She was no longer the inexperienced adolescent who had cringed before Gaveston but a mature woman who could use her attractions and her wits to gain her ends.

Her wits served her well. When Despencer and the King robbed her of her estates and put her under the surveillance of the favourite's wife, Eleanor de Clare, on the grounds that Isabelle was the sister of the French king, with whom England was on the verge of war, the Queen remained silent. When a rumour was whispered through the court that the King was planning to divorce her, Isabelle made no protest. So well did she maintain her outward calm and her politeness towards Despencer that he and Edward thought her too docile to be dangerous. But the Queen was prepared to seize her chance.

It came in 1325 when, unsuspecting, Edward sent her to France to negotiate on his behalf with her brother. Rumours may have come to the English Court of the party of Edward's disaffected subjects which was gathering around Isabelle (whose support she had been canvassing for years, with the utmost secrecy), but the King still trusted his wife sufficiently to send her their eldest son, his namesake, to be his proxy in performing homage to the French king for their Continental estates.

With this obvious advantage, Isabelle could now afford to show her hand. She began openly to plot treason against Edward, and flaunted her adultery with one of the exiles, the Marcher Lord Roger Mortimer, who had been defeated in his war with Despencer in Wales and who had, in 1323, escaped from the Tower of London, probably with Isabelle's connivance or at least her foreknowledge.

When Edward demanded that his wife return to England forthwith, she replied with a decisive refusal:

> I feel that marriage is a joining together of man and woman, maintaining the undivided habit of life, and that someone has come between my husband and myself trying to break this bond; I protest that I will not return until this intruder is removed, but, discarding my marriage garment, shall assume the robes of widow-hood and mourning until I am revenged.[3]

This challenge issued, the Queen and Mortimer left her brother's Court (where she was no longer welcome) and found refuge with Count William of Hainault. With his help (bought by promise of marriage between her elder son and the Count's daughter), Isabelle mounted an army and on 23 September 1326 embarked for the invasion of England.

While Mortimer directed the military campaign, Isabelle's own manœuvres were masterly. She assumed, as she had threatened, widow's weeds, and with a pretty show of piety made a pilgrimage to the shrine of Bury St Edmunds. Her support grew daily.

Soon after King Edward had fled into the west, taking the Despencers, father and son, with him, London welcomed the Queen. With a vast army behind her, she followed him and on 26 October entered Bristol. There the elder Despencer was forced to surrender: he was swiftly executed.

The King panicked. He and Despencer embarked for Ireland, were driven back by adverse winds onto the Welsh coast and then fled into the hinterland. They were found at the Abbey of Neath on 16 November. While Edward was escorted, under heavy guard, to Kenilworth Castle, Hugh Despencer was put on trial. Among the charges were those of disparaging the Queen, procuring the death of the late Earl of Lancaster, taking unwarranted rewards for himself and his father at the expense of rightful claimants, dishonouring the King by inducing him to abandon his kingdom. Inevitably, he was found guilty; inevitably, sentence of death was passed and executed.

Never before had a queen consort usurped the government of the realm, even though Isabelle gave her usurpation a semblance of legality by ruling in the name of her husband. Nor had a queen ever openly taken a lover. In fact, before her there is only one instance of a queen's infidelity, and that not well substantiated: it is alleged that Isabelle of Angoulême, King John's second wife, once took a lover—but only one, for the King had him and his two accomplices killed, and their bodies hung over the Queen's bed as a warning against future adultery.

Isabelle failed to obtain Edward's consent to the deed of abdication with which he was presented, but in the Parliament which she called, using the King's Great Seal, there were few willing to raise their voices in support of so unpopular a monarch. So numerous and so serious were the charges levelled against Edward II that the Articles of Deposition were, on the whole, enthusiastically upheld. When they were read to Edward, in his prison, he broke down and agreed to abdicate, fearful lest (as Isabelle threatened) England should repudiate his son as well as himself and set up Mortimer in their place. If he also hoped, by this capitulation, to save his own life, the former King was to be sadly disappointed.

On 21 September 1327 England learned that Edward, one-time King of England, was dead.

Queen Isabelle played her part to the end, attending her late husband's funeral in suitable black and grief. There was nothing about her to suggest that she, and her lover, had ordered Edward's death, though rumours were even then rife to that effect. Nor was there any mark on the corpse to suggest foul play, neither the wound of sword or dagger nor any sign that he had been poisoned. But the rumour-mongers suggested a method of murder which would account for this, saying that if the body were opened up, burn marks would be found, in "those parts in which he had been wont to take his vicious pleasure", into which hot irons had been inserted by the murderers employed by the woman whom they were now calling 'the she-wolf of France'.

Queen Isabelle's triumph did not last long. Roger Mortimer was already unpopular as ever Gaveston and Despencer had been, especially after his ignominious part in the arrangement of a peace with Scotland, detrimental to English prestige and government, which was signed at Northampton in 1328. Nor had Mortimer and his mistress taken any care to endear themselves to the new king, the sixteen-year-old Edward III, who retained some respect for his dead father and who resented the control of his mother's lover over his person and his government.

In October 1330 Mortimer was arrested by order of the King, and inevitably met death as a traitor. Isabelle was not brought to trial, nor was she imprisoned, but she lived out her life under surveillance in luxurious seclusion, assuaging her conscience—if conscience she had—with good works. She died in 1358.

For more than twenty years, 1307–30, the sexuality of a king and queen of England had played a decisive part in the politics of the kingdom, bringing both to ultimate ruin. But it was not their sexuality intrinsically which brought about these calamities: rather the combination of it with the political ambitions and pretensions of their lovers. It was a theme to be repeated in later centuries, though never with so dire a result.

3

The Service of Venus

Noble ladies of the Middle Ages may have been discouraged from dishonouring their marital bed, but they did not hesitate to take nominal lovers in the courtly tradition.

The concept of 'courtly love' was an offshoot of the chivalric code which bound together the knights of Europe in a brotherhood which transcended, though it did not negate, national loyalties. Chivalry was a convention of class and of the military life—the rules of the game by which the fierce contentions of European issues were fought, and which in peacetime provided the ritual and ceremony then (and even now) dear to male sensibilities.

The military life provided no role for the womenfolk of the knights and war-lords, but, once the latter had accumulated land won in war, the matter of producing a son to inherit was always a priority. Women were also valued when a male line failed, and the rival bids of sister-heiresses took up much of the time of medieval law-courts. But beyond the claims to respect of motherhood and inheritance, women were low in the scheme of things in the Middle Ages, allowed no voice in government, no role in public life beyond the ornamental. It was only when the troubadours of southern France brought into England the concept of woman as a social being, a softening influence, that women were accorded privileges—if not rights.

Marital love was still regarded with some embarrassment, almost as a defiling of the sacred bond tied in the wedding ceremony; but the delightful, romantic concept of the knight and his chosen lady caught the popular imagination and came to figure largely in aristocratic literature and Court life from the twelfth even to the sixteenth century.

The theory was that a knight should choose a lady—almost invariably a married woman—for whom he must sigh and moon in a sweat of unrequited love. That the object of his affection should be already married was a necessary precaution, for the courtly love tradition admitted, in theory, no physical relations: an unmarried girl would be liable to scandal under such conditions, but a matron was generally supposed to be beyond temptation. A lady might condescend to favour the knight who wooed her, but her graciousness was bounded within strict limits: she might receive verses and small tokens from her swain but her own generosity must never go further than the bestowal of a 'colour', a ribbon or scarf which the knight would carry into battle or tournament to bring her honour in his victory.

The tournament was, in fact, one of the main manifestations of courtly romance. These mock battles might be formal jousts, with lances safely covered, or they might be the dangerous mêlées in which men were often wounded, even killed, but they were generally conducted in a festival atmosphere, with music and pageantry, and were a welcome opportunity for women to show themselves off, seated in the spectators' loges, while the men fought to do them honour.

In many instances, knight and lady may have ventured beyond the convention of mutual admiration, of breast-heavings for the desired and unobtainable sweetheart, but if they did, there is little concrete evidence of it. A husband well-versed in the convention would not object to having his wife admired by another man (besides, he probably had a lady of his own to woo—and his choice of his serfs' daughters for more tangible dalliance); but he would object to his wife making a fool of him. Perhaps many a husband held his tongue when he discovered that his wife and her knight had cuckolded him, lest he himself become a laughing-stock in the war camp; only open gossip would rile him to take revenge.

The courtly love convention did much to raise the social status of women, though for hundreds of years aristocratic ladies would continue to be valued primarily for their fortunes and their ability to produce (male) children. However, romantic idealism does not seem to have made kings more temperate.

King Edward III was one of the most enthusiastic exponents of courtly love, as part of the trappings of chivalry. He revived the idea of the Arthurian Round Table, taking his lords and knights as brothers-in-arms on equal terms within the code: courtesy to ladies, the protection of widows and orphans, were part of the chivalric order—though it applied, seemingly, only among gentlefolk: the peasantry were still negligible possessions to be coerced and persecuted with impunity.

The famous Order of the Garter is said to have resulted from a piece of chivalric gallantry by Edward III. The Countess of Salisbury, dancing at a Court ball, lost her garter, and, to spare her blushes from the sniggers of courtiers, the King picked it up, with the immortal words *"Honi soit qui mal y pense"*, "Evil to him who evil thinks", declaring that the garter should become the symbol of the most honourable of England's orders of knights (as it is to this day).

Contemporaries asserted that the King tried to make the Countess of Salisbury his mistress, for all his vaunted ideals. He released her from siege in her castle in the north, it was said, was overcome by her beauty and tried to tempt her into adultery. The Countess utterly refused him, at which he remembered his honour and admired her the more.

In fact, Edward seems, for the most part of his married life, to have been devoted to his wife, Philippa of Hainault. It was a love-match, contemporaries said: Edward had been bidden by his mother, Isabelle of France, to choose one of the daughters of William of Hainault to seal her bargain with him which was to provide the cash to raise an army against Edward II; from the Count's several daughters, the boy had chosen Philippa. Certainly, the fact that the couple were rarely parted in the four decades of their marriage seems to validate the theory: when the King visited his foreign dominions or went to war, Philippa almost invariably accompanied him, at a time when royal ladies were usually left safely at home.

It was only in the last years of the King's life that he took a mistress—in his dotage, it was said, though he was still only in his mid-sixties when he died in 1377. But Edward's mistress, Alice Perrers, was to cause unprecedented scandal and diminish the prestige of the Crown.

Her origins are much disputed: some sources say that she was the daughter of the powerful churchman William of Wykeham, others that she was the daughter of a Devon weaver or an Essex tiler, but it is unlikely that the illegitimate daughter of a bishop, let alone an artisan's child, should become a maid-of-honour at Court, as Alice did during Queen Philippa's last years (her fellow-maids were all of good if not noble blood):

most probably she came of the Hertfordshire family of gentry surnamed Perrers.

Alice appears in Philippa's will, in 1369, as "the beloved damsel Alicia de Preston" (the identification, though on the surface dubious, has been accepted by many historians), to whom the Queen bequeathed ten marks a year, to be paid at Easter and Michaelmas. That Alice was already Edward III's mistress by the time of Philippa's death seems eminently likely, for above the pension left her by the Queen, she received "all the jewels, goods and chattels that the said Queen left in the hands of Euphemia, wife of Sir William de Heserlarton, knight, and the said Euphemia is to deliver them to the said Alice on the receipt of this command",[1] which was issued by the King's clerks.

In the years that followed, Alice Perrers acquired ever more wealth from her generous lover, and the widower King treated her as if she were his queen. In 1374 he gave a seven-day tournament in her honour, at which she appeared gaily dressed and dazzlingly bejewelled, to preside as 'Lady of the Sun' throughout the festivities. More rewarding than her decorative role, however, was the part which Alice Perrers began to play in the administration of royal government: it was later alleged that she took her seat on the judges' benches in the law courts, to bring pressure on them to decide in her favour where cases touched her own (extensive) property or the interests of her protégés—many of whom, it was said, had purchased her influence.

In May 1376 the "Good Parliament" voiced many criticisms of royal government, taking advantage of the fact that the King himself was too mortally ill to rebuff them with his former sternness, and among their grievances were those that Alice had "been preferred in the King's love before the Queen" and that she had "pursued diverse business and quarrels in the Courts of the King, by way of maintenance, and for pay and having part". By then Edward III had shed all the magnificent dignity and strength of his youth and feebly submitted to Parliament's demand that his mistress should be banished from the realm.

Alice, however, did not capitulate. She did not go into exile but, as soon as she was able, crept back to Westminster. Nevertheless, her day was over: in June 1377 her 'protector' died. As soul and body parted, the royal mistress fell on the corpse, ripping off Edward's rings, her last wages, before she fled from Court. Before the end of the year she was once again arraigned and now deprived of her ill-gotten-gains in land and money.

Alice Perrers had three children, but whether they were the King's or begotten by her husband Sir William de Windsor, or any other man's, it is impossible to determine. She had married de Windsor some three years before Edward's death, while she was certainly the King's mistress, so perhaps the knight was merely an obedient royal servant, ready to cover Alice with his good name in return for reward. After 1377, Alice Perrers was not persecuted further, but lived until 1400, repeatedly asserting her rights to the property which had been confiscated.

Many historians have suggested that the pen-portrait of Lady Meed in Langland's *Piers Plowman* was an eye-witness's impression of Alice Perrers. Certainly it is feasible that this Londoner-poet may have seen her in the days of her triumphant beauty. He wrote:

> Her robe fur-edged, the finest on earth,
> Crowned with a crown, the King hath no better,
> Fairly her fingers were fretted with rings,
> And in the rings red rubies, as red as a furnace,
> And diamonds of dearest price, and double sapphires,
> Sapphires and beryls, poison to destroy.
> Her rich robe of scarlet dye,
> Her ribbons set with gold, red gold, rare stones;
> Her array ravished me; such riches saw I never;
> I wondered who she was, and whose wife she were.
> 'What is this woman,' said I, 'so wonderfully clad?'

His companion replied:

> '. . . That is Meed the maid; she oft hath harmed me,
> She hath slandered my love that is named Loyalty,
> And belied her to lords that have the laws to keep.'[2]

It is also possible that Geoffrey Chaucer took Alice Perrers as the model for Alice in the Miller's story which is among his *Canterbury Tales*. Chaucer was a courtier in the last years of Edward III, and like Langland may have seen her often:

> She was a pretty creature, fair and tender,
> And had a weasel's body, softly slender. . . .
> She wore a broad silk fillet rather high
> And certainly she had a lecherous eye.

And she had plucked her eyebrows into bows,
Slenderly arched they were, and black as sloes. . . .
She had a shining colour, gaily tinted,
And brighter than a florin newly minted. . . .
Her mouth was sweet as mead or honey—say
A hoard of apples lying in the hay. . . .
She was a daisy, O a lollypop
For any nobleman to take to bed.
Or some good man of yeoman stock to wed.[3]

On the other hand, it may be that Chaucer was describing his (presumed) sister-in-law, Catherine Roet, a married woman (Lady Swynford) who was for years the mistress of Edward III's third son John of Gaunt, Duke of Lancaster, and who bore him four children while he was still married to the Spanish Princess Constance. After the Duchess of Lancaster's death, John of Gaunt married Catherine, and Richard II legitimised their children. The Beauforts, as Lancaster's former bastards were named, were awarded titles and estates: two of them became earls, one rose high in the Church hierarchy, and the only daughter married a powerful northern magnate.

Despite the fact that Gaunt had, albeit belatedly, 'made an honest woman' of Catherine, the proud ladies of the Court would not accept the new Duchess, roundly declaring that they "would not come into no place where she should be present; and, moreover, they said, it should be great shame for them that such a duchess, come of so base a blood, and concubine to the Duke in his other wives' days, should go and have pre-eminence before them".[4]

Catherine's blood was not base: she has been identified as the daughter of Sir Payn Roet, the Guienne herald, and as the wife of a Lincolnshire knight, and may well have been the sister of Philippa la Picarde, a former lady-in-waiting to Queen Philippa, who married the poet Chaucer. It was not Catherine's parentage which the Court ladies resented so much as the threat which her career posed to respectable married women who would not care to be in the same position as the Duke of Lancaster's late wife Constance.

In fact, throughout the Middle Ages, public opinion was not usually outraged by a man's infidelity unless it impinged on his public life or on the sacred ties of marriage, especially when it promoted divorce. A few years earlier than the Lancaster

marriage, there had been another scandal at Court when Richard
II's favourite, Robert de Vere, became so infatuated with Agnes
Lancecrona, a maid-of-honour of Richard's queen, that he
actually requested a divorce from his wife in the papal courts.
The King's support of the illicit love affair was much reviled,
especially as de Vere's wife was Richard's own cousin Philippa
de Coucy. For a time there was a good deal of ill-feeling in the
royal family about it.

Later, some thirty years after the marriage of Lancaster and
Catherine Swynford, the Court was shocked when Humphrey,
Duke of Gloucester, uncle of the child-king Henry VI, repudiated his wife to marry his mistress. This was Eleanor Cobham,
one of Duchess Jacqueline of Gloucester's ladies-in-waiting, and
she was living openly with the Duke long before his divorce.
They had two children before their union was legalised in 1428.
The resentment against Duchess Eleanor must have been much
like that against Duchess Catherine earlier, for when she was ac-
cused of witchcraft in 1441, she won no sympathy, had no
friends to defend her. Eleanor Cobham was found guilty of using
the black arts to "determine the succession to the throne"—that
is, to put her husband in his nephew's place. She was forced to
do public penance for her crime and to spend the rest of her life
in custody.

After Alice Perrers, there was not, for years, any woman who
used her place with a king to aggrandise herself or influence
politics. But Margaret of Anjou, wife of the weak (or saintly)
King Henry VI, may well have taken as her lovers such men
as the Dukes of Suffolk and Somerset to control government
through them. Contemporary critics certainly charged her
with this, and Henry VI did not help his wife's reputation by
his amazement at the birth of her son, apparently unaware, in
his other-worldly haze, that he had begotten a child by her:
but the evidence is confused, and the charges against Queen
Margaret's virtue may be merely a by-product of the general
distaste for a woman's meddling in politics.

Since Henry I there had surely been no such lover of women
as King Edward IV, the tall, sinewy (until he went fat in middle
age) and floridly handsome usurper of Henry VI's throne.
Edward of York was a fine specimen of manhood: his rank only
enhanced his attraction in women's eyes. Tales about his sexual
appetite and prowess surpassed even those told of the riotous

youth of Henry V, who 'fervently followed the service of Venus as well as of Mars; as a young man he burned her torches, and other insolences accompanied the years of his untamed youth"[5] (though none of Henry's mistresses is named).

Edward IV was the darling of the ladies of London and, contemporaries claimed, several of them shared his bed. "He was licentious in the extreme," wrote an Italian visitor to Edward's Court, "moreover, it was said that he had been most insolent to numerous women after he had seduced them, for, as soon as he grew weary of dalliance, he gave up the ladies, much against their will, to the other courtiers. He pursued with no discrimination the married and unmarried, the noble and lowly: however, he took none by force."[6]

Still, Edward acknowledged only three of his bastards: Arthur Plantagenet became a trusted royal servant and was created Viscount Lisle by Henry VIII—he was the son of Elizabeth Lacy, who also produced a daughter, Elizabeth, who became the ancestress of the earls of Peterborough. Another daughter, Grace (by an unknown mother) was probably brought up by the King's wife, Elizabeth Woodville, for she was numbered among the Queen's ladies in her funeral cortége in 1492.

In his youth, Edward may have used the time-honoured ploy of pretending to marry a woman when he could win her no other way. Some time after the King's death, evidence came to light that he had married the widowed Lady Eleanor Butler, a daughter of the Earl of Shrewsbury, which, if true, would have invalidated his later marriage to Elizabeth Woodville and put his children out of the line of succession to the throne by their illegitimacy. The story may have been a fabrication on behalf of Edward's brother, Richard of Gloucester, who in 1483 claimed the throne for himself, setting aside Edward's children; on the other hand, Edward (not yet the king at the time of the wedding) may have gone through some sort of ceremony with Eleanor, the 'troth-plighting' so common in the Middle Ages, which was nearly as solemn as the marriage service itself but which was regarded as less binding if there was no proof of consummation.

Edward may have used such a promise to break down Eleanor's resistance to him—"he took none by force", as it was said; he may sincerely have intended to marry her. Perhaps it was her inability to give him children which cooled his ardour, for even then Edward was vying for the crown, and sons were a vital adjunct to a king's security in power.

When Edward (king since 1460) married Elizabeth Woodville in 1464, he had long since tired of Eleanor Butler (who died in 1468). Like Eleanor, Elizabeth was somewhat older than he; like Eleanor, she was a widow; unlike her predecessor, Elizabeth Woodville was already a mother, with two sons by her late husband. As the King said, when he broke the news of his marriage to his mother, Elizabeth "is a widow and hath already children; by God's blessing, I am a bachelor and have some too; and so each of us hath a proof that neither of us is like to be barren".[7]

Apparently, so desirous had the King been of Elizabeth's body that for once he had attempted force, but "when Edward placed a dagger at her throat, to make her submit to his passion, she remained unperturbed, determined to die rather than live unchastely with the King"[8]—or having an eye to the main chance of becoming queen. Only by marriage would Elizabeth Woodville be won. Even then, their wedding was kept secret for some months, until just before Michaelmas 1464: Edward was supposedly wooing a foreign princess for the sake of international diplomacy at that time. Only when she was known to be pregnant did he acknowledge Elizabeth as his queen, risking offending the French king, whose sister-in-law was intended for his bride, to stake all on his wife's giving birth to a son and heir. In the event, in February 1466 the Queen gave the King a daughter, but in the years that followed she produced five more daughters and two sons.

Marriage did not curb Edward's enthusiasm for amorous escapades: he was by nature polygamous. "The King would say that he had three concubines", it was reported on good authority, "one the merriest, another the wiliest, the third the holiest harlot in his realm."[9] Who the wiliest and holiest harlots were remains a mystery, but the merriest was Jane Shore, "in whom the King therefore took especial pleasure. For many he had, but her he loved . . .".[10]

Though this gleeful harlot is famed as Jane Shore in history and fable, opera and stage-play, she was born Elizabeth Lambert, the daughter of a London merchant, and became Elizabeth Shore on her marriage. As the saintly Thomas More (who may have seen her in her old age) reported, Jane Shore was "born in London, worshipfully friended, honestly brought up and very well married, saving somewhat too soon; her husband [was] an honest citizen, young and goodly, and of good substance".[11] She was not beautiful, he thought, but "delighted not men so much in her beauty as in her pleasant behaviour, for a proper wit had she and could both read well and write [at a time when female literacy was quite rare]; merry in company, ready and quick of answer, neither mute nor full of babble; sometimes taunting without displeasure and not without disport".[12]

At the death of Edward IV in 1484, Jane Shore did not return to her husband (whom she had divorced in 1476) but remained at Court as the mistress of her late lover's stepson the Earl of Dorset and then of one of Edward's boon companions, Lord Chamberlain Hastings. This was at the time when the Queen's Woodville relations were attempting to seize power as the guardians of the child-king Edward V: against them was ranged the late King's brother, Richard of Gloucester. For all their former rivalry, Queen Elizabeth and Jane Shore worked together to prevent Richard's usurpation, but they failed. When Richard III took the throne, one of his first victims was Hastings; reputedly, he spent the night before his execution in the arms of Jane Shore.

Although Richard III had not a blameless reputation (he is known to have had at least two illegitimate sons), the wantonness of his late brother's Court had apparently shocked him. Now he brought Jane Shore to account, with the Church authorities charged to demand her public penance: walking the streets of London clad only in her shift and carrying a candle. Then she went into Ludgate prison.

There is a curious letter from Richard III to Bishop Russell of Lincoln, of 1484, which deals with the fate of Jane Shore. The King wrote:

Right reverend father in God, etc.,

Signifying unto you that it is showed unto us that our servant and solicitor Thomas Lynom, marvellously blinded and abused with the late wife of William Shore, now living in Ludgate by our commandment, hath made contract of matrimony with her, as it is said, and intendeth to our full great marvel to effect the same.

We, for many causes, would be sorry that he should be so disposed; pray you therefore to send for him and in that ye

4

The Concubine

Alice Perrers and Jane Shore were the nearest approximation in England to the *maîtresses-en-titre* of the French kings, but even they did not aspire to the eminence which their French counterparts enjoyed. Agnes Sorel, Charles VIII's powerful and unpopular mistress (poisoned by her enemies), Anne, Duchesse d'Estampes, the most renowned of the many mistresses of François I, and Diane de Poitiers, Duchesse de Valentinois, who ruled the Court of Henri II, began a tradition which culminated in the eighteenth century with the reigns of Mesdames de Pompadour and du Barry. These great ladies were openly hailed as their king's favourites; they paraded in queenly magnificence; their influence was sought above that of the neglected royal wives; they made their mark in the politics of the day.

However, not one of them would play such a significant role in her nation's history as Anne Boleyn, mistress, then wife, of Henry VIII, played in England's.

For all his later reputation, as a young man Henry Tudor was remarkably chaste and innocent. He had been brought up under his father's eye, educated and governed by staid, sober old men, guarded from all the temptations usually held out to young princes. When he came to the throne, in 1509, he was eighteen years old and still unmarried.

But Henry soon remedied that: less than two months after his accession he married Catherine of Aragon, widow of his brother Arthur, Prince of Wales (who had died in 1502). It was said to be a love-match, but, sentiment apart, it was a useful alliance in terms of international relations.

For a while, in the first years of the reign, it seemed that Henry and Catherine would provide the kingdom with a model of domestic piety. The gay, accomplished and lively King paid affectionate attention to his wife (a few years his senior), and for some time he looked no further than his wife's bed for sexual satisfaction. One living son was born to the couple, on 1 January 1512, but he died less than two months later, and though Queen Catherine thereafter had no trouble in conceiving, she suffered several miscarriages and, even when she went her full term, four out of her five children were stillborn: the only survivor was a daughter, Mary, not the son for whom Henry VIII prayed.

A somewhat garbled tale has come down to us of the first woman whose name was linked with the King's—apparently as early as 1514, while Catherine of Aragon was still trying to achieve motherhood. The Spanish ambassador (friend of Queen Catherine) gathered information to the effect that Henry had been paying court to one Lady Anne Hastings, a married woman, sister of the Duke of Buckingham. The King had used one of his grooms of the Bedchamber, Sir Henry Compton, to address her, but Compton was so indiscreet as to approach Anne in the presence of her sharp-eyed sister Elizabeth, Lady Fitzwalter. Fearing for the family honour (or perhaps jealous?), the latter had gone to Buckingham with the story, and he had himself come upon Anne and Compton together. Whether the King's emissary was using the opportunity of his master's messages for personal dalliance with Lady Anne seems unclear but probable. Hastings, who was informed of his wife's misdemeanours, swept her off to a convent sixty miles away—to the fury of Henry VIII, who turned Buckingham and the Fitzwalters out of his household.

Now he turned against his wife too, suspecting that every woman in her retinue was a spy on him, as Lady Fitzwalter had been, "such as go about the palace insidiously, spying out every unwatched movement in order to tell the Queen stories . . .".[1] As the Spanish ambassador was told, "the King would have liked to have turned them all out, only it appeared too great a scandal. Afterwards almost all the Court knew the Queen had been vexed with the King, and the King with her, and thus the storm continued".[2]

Never again did Catherine of Aragon know real peace of mind, though he was kind to and appreciative of her almost until the end of their life as husband and wife. There can be no doubt that she was sincerely in love with Henry, even to the end of her life, after years of cruel usage and misery.

Among the several (mainly anonymous) mistresses of the King

after the incident of 1514 was a remarkable Flemish woman, Jane Popincourt. When she had arrived at the English Court is not known, but she may have been the French teacher engaged for Henry's sisters in 1498. The first definite reference to her is as the mistress of the Duc de Longueville, a French hostage lodged in the royal household in the early years of Henry VIII's reign, but by 1514 Jane's amatory reputation was such that, when she was mooted as a maid-of-honour for the King's sister Mary, who was going to France to marry King Louis XII, the French king himself struck her name from the list, swearing that he would rather see the infamous woman burned than attending his innocent bride. Jane therefore remained in England, reputedly as Henry VIII's mistress, until after Louis's death on the last day of 1514, whereupon, with £100 in her pocket as payment for her services, she embarked for France and the welcoming arms of de Longueville.

By 1518 the woman highest in royal favour was the young Elizabeth Blount, still a teenager if her birth-date of 1500, surmised by historians, is correct. She had come to Court in 1512 from her home in Shropshire, under the patronage of her kinsman Lord Mountjoy (a member of Queen Catherine's intimate circle, having married Ines de Venegas, one of her Spanish maids-of-honour).

Soon 'Bessie' Blount was one of the belles of the Court, excelling in "singing, dancing and all goodly pastimes", according to the chronicler Hall. Her talents were certainly put on display, for time and again she appeared in the newly fashionable Court masques-fancy-dress entertainment which had come to England from the great Courts of Renaissance Europe, combining singing and dancing with spectacular staging. Bessie was one of four 'ladies of Savoy' who partnered four 'knights from Portugal' (one of them the King) in a masque at Greenwich at Christmas 1513. So delighted with the entertainment was Queen Catherine (who was always a spectator, never a dancer herself) that she had them repeat the performance in her own chamber by torchlight. But then Bessie Blount was not yet the King's mistress. She may not have caught his eye until 1518, six years after she came to Court.

In the early summer of 1519 Elizabeth Blount gave the King what Queen Catherine could never supply: a living, healthy son. Henry Fitzroy, as the baby was named, was "a goodly man-child, in beauty like to the father and the mother".[3] He was born at the Priory of St Lawrence at Blackmore in Essex, where in later years his mother lived with her husband Gilbert Talboys.

The date of Bessie's marriage cannot be dated exactly, but it seems likely that the wedding took place in the summer of 1522, for in June of that year the couple received a royal grant of the manor of Rokeby in Warwickshire, which may have formed part of the dowry which the King awarded his mistress. Certainly it seems probable that Talboys was chosen by Henry to marry Bessie, for the young man's marriage was in his gift, as a ward in Chancery. Thereafter Elizabeth no longer figured at Court, and though the King always doted on his son, the mother had no further claim on him. At New Year, Lady Talboys, like other titled ladies, would receive a gift of plate from the King— in January 1532 he sent her "a gilt goblet with a cover"—but by providing her with a husband, Henry VIII had paid any debt he owed his mistress.

After Talboys' death, Bessie rose still higher in the social scale by marrying Edward, Lord Clinton (probably some twelve years her junior), and she lived on until 1540. She had not done badly for one of eleven children of a Shropshire knight.

The King might rear his son as a prince; he might create him Duke of Richmond and Somerset and award him such powerful offices as those of Lord High Admiral, Lord Warden of the Marches and Lord Lieutenant of Ireland; he might boast that he would marry him to a princess of Denmark or Portugal, but there was no gainsaying the fact that Henry Fitzroy was the King's bastard, not his legitimate heir. How dearly would Henry have loved to have named his son as his successor instead of the one daughter, Mary, who survived Catherine of Aragon's many pregnancies. It was mooted at one point that the Pope might be approached to sanction Fitzroy's marriage to his half-sister, that together they might rule England one day; at another, it was suggested that Henry VIII award him the kingdom of Ireland. But every plan came to nothing. Henry Fitzroy grew up healthy (but for the strain of consumption still dormant, which killed him in his teens), intelligent and lively: a continual reminder to Henry VIII that he had no legitimate male heir to succeed him.

The safe transfer of the crown was a matter of supreme

importance to the King. His own father, Henry VII, had come to the throne because there was no indisputable heir of the Plantagenet line to be king; what Henry VII had taken by force from Richard III and ratified by dubious constitutional measures, could be challenged by any pretender if Henry VIII could not ensure a peaceful succession by providing an heir of unimpeachable quality. He had his daughter Mary, it was true, but England had never had a queen regnant before, apart from that determined Matilda, Henry I's daughter, who had claimed the crown in the twelfth century, but she had never been able to wrest the kingdom from her usurping cousin Stephen. It was by no means certain that Englishmen of the sixteenth century would be more amenable than their ancestors had been to female rule. Henry VIII could well foresee just such another anarchy as that of the Stephen–Matilda wars, or a return to the chaos of the more recent Wars of the Roses, if he—or rather, his wife—could not give the Crown a male heir.

Romantic biographers have liked to suggest that Henry VIII divorced Catherine of Aragon for love of Anne Boleyn, to make her his wife. This is not true. Henry had considered divorcing Catherine long before he became ensnared in Anne's charms, but he had never put his plans into action. The King's decision was firmly grounded in his fears of a war of the royal succession after his death and his intention of fathering a child on a new wife: Anne Boleyn's refusal to become his mistress only intensified Henry's desire to marry again, to marry Anne, and galvanised him into action.

From both sides of her family Anne Boleyn had inherited an ambition and drive which sustained her in her long climb to the consort's throne. The Boleyns had been tradesmen in the fifteenth century until one of their number amassed a fortune, won election as Lord Mayor of London and retired to live out his life as a country gentleman. Three generations of Boleyn men had married heiresses, the most recent, Sir Thomas, had even aspired to wed Lady Elizabeth Howard, sister of the Duke of Norfolk. And for generations, throughout the sixteenth century and into the seventeenth, the Howards proved time and again that their ruling passion was ambition. They plotted and conspired, intrigued and bargained, for their self-aggrandisement, many of them suffering traitors' deaths for their pretensions. Anne was the daughter of Sir Thomas Boleyn and Lady Elizabeth Howard, inheritor of the traits of both families.

Less strong a character was her elder sister Mary, the first of the family to attract the attention of Henry VIII. Like Anne, Mary had served her apprenticeship in courtly accomplishments and sexual adventure in France, as maid-of-honour to the French queen. She was any man's for the taking, it seems: the not-too-fastidious King François I called her "a hackney". Mary returned to England in about 1522, to take service with Catherine of Aragon; her liaison with King Henry followed swiftly and lasted about two years.

Mary Boleyn had children, but they may have been begotten by her husband William Carey (his knighthood by the King was one of the few rewards she received for her services); certainly, Henry never acknowledged them or advanced them as he did Henry Fitzroy.

Anne Boleyn, coming from France with unsullied reputation, was more prudent than her sister. She rebuffed Henry's first advances and for years refused to become his mistress, despite the King's urgent pleas. She would not give herself, as Mary had done, without assurance that she would reap some worthwhile reward. Clearly Anne saw Henry VIII's need of a legitimate son and, seemingly with cold determination, played on that obsession and his lust for herself in order to win a consort's crown.

> Beseeching you with all my heart to let me know definitely your whole intention touching the love between us two [wrote Henry in one of the many fervent love-letters he addressed to Anne] . . . if it pleases you to do the duty of a true, loyal mistress and friend, and to give yourself body and heart to me, who will be (and have been) your very loyal servant (if your strictness does not forbid me), I promise you that not only the name will be due to you, but also to take you for my sole mistress, rejecting all others except yourself out of mind and affection, and to serve you alone. . . .[4]

But Anne would not yield. By the beginning of 1527, Henry had come to the conclusion that the only way he might possess her was by marriage.

In fact, the King's conscience genuinely troubled him, that he had sinned by marrying Catherine, the wife of his dead brother—there was a biblical text to prove it (if one ignored another which expressly commanded it); he felt that God was punishing him for that sin by denying him a son. By ridding himself of Catherine, he could marry Anne and beget a son with God's blessing. But first he had to obtain the Pope's blessing, to procure a divorce—that is, more accurately, an annulment; for the Church would agree to the parting of husband and wife only if it could be proved that the marriage had never been legal in the first place. There were several arguments for divorce at that time: it might be shown that one of the parties had been betrothed to another person before the marriage, and that betrothal had never been satisfactorily terminated; it might be demonstrated that one of the parties had married below the age of consent or had been coerced by a parent into the marriage against their will; or, and this was the usual pretext, the plaintiff might bring evidence that he or she was related to the defendant within the "forbidden degrees" of consanguinity (which stretched as far as fifth cousins). Henry VIII, in fact, could make out a good case for the illegality of his marriage to Catherine of Aragon: she had been first married to his elder brother, a relationship well within the prohibited degrees of kinship. At the time of Henry and Catherine's wedding, the King had taken care to obtain from the then Pope a dispensation permitting the match, on the grounds that Catherine and Prince Arthur had never consummated their marriage, but now Henry and his lawyers put forward the argument that Catherine had lied when she had claimed, back in 1509, that she came to him a virgin, that the dispensation was based on that false oath and was therefore invalid, as was the marriage.

Under normal circumstances the King of England might have felt reasonably certain of obtaining his divorce. It was not unknown for one pope to set aside the ruling of a former pope. But he had chosen the wrong moment to lodge his petition in the papal courts, for, in May 1527, just as Henry was preparing his case, Rome was sacked by the forces of Queen Catherine's nephew, the Emperor Charles V, who took Pope Clement VII prisoner. There was little likelihood that the captive would award Henry a divorce which would shame and depose his captor's aunt.

On 22 June 1527 Henry told Catherine that he felt bound, by his conscience and on the advice of his councillors, to seek a divorce. She was too horrified and bewildered to reply, but burst into tears. Then, and later, the King tried to comfort her, to cajole Catherine into admitting that their marriage had been illegal and thereby help his case. But no argument of duty to the Crown or personal honour would sway the Queen from her declaration that her marriage to Henry was, and always had been, valid.

The King was not a patient man. Once he realised that the Queen would not yield, he gave up arguing with her and ignored her completely. Catherine was neglected and isolated in her own Court, while Anne queened it in fine clothes and jewels, the centre of every festivity, courted by every aspirant to royal favour.

But months passed, years passed, while Rome vacillated and Henry stormed. Anne became tense and nervous, her temper always on the brink of snapping—but still she held out. By the last months of 1532 it was obvious that Cardinal Campeggio, whom the Pope had sent to hear the divorce case (with instructions to temporise as long as possible) had no intention of granting the King his freedom.

Then Henry VIII took matters into his own hands. He denied the validity of papal authority in England and had his Archbishop of Canterbury, Thomas Cranmer, pronounce the divorce on his own authority.

Simplistic accounts of the reign contend that Anne Boleyn was the cause of the Reformation of the Church in England under Henry VIII, but that is a perversion of the truth. The King's desire to marry Anne was obviously a contributory factor in his breach with Rome and subsequent establishment of a Church ruled by English bishops and Parliament under the supremacy of the sovereign; but there were many other factors in that step, equally if not more urgent: the King's need to remarry and beget a male heir; his increasing unwillingness to pay tribute, fiscal and juridical, to a foreign potentate such as 'the Bishop of Rome', and so on. In no way did Henry subscribe to the doctrines of the Protestant reformers who were harassing the Church on the Continent: he had, in fact, some years earlier denounced the heresies of Martin Luther in a work of theology from his own pen; the only tenet of the Protestants which received his agreement was their denial of papal authority. Many of Henry's subjects were doctrinal Protestants, and in the years that followed they would bring pressure to bear to have

Queen Isabelle, 'the she-wolf of France', and her army encamped before Hereford in November 1326. In the background Edward II's 'minion', Hugh Despencer, is executed.

Jane Shore, the 'merriest' of Edward IV's mistresses.

Anne Boleyn, mistress then second wife of Henry VIII.

the new 'Church of England' take on a more Protestant complexion in doctrine and ritual, but with little success while Henry VIII lived. Anne Boleyn is said to have had Lutheran sympathies, but there is nothing to prove that or to suggest that she used her influence with Henry in an attempt to change the doctrines of the established Church.

After years of withstanding the King's pleas for her body, Anne Boleyn had given herself to him some months before his divorce from Catherine. What made her do so then, when for so long she had refused to yield? It is possible that she feared that Henry was tiring of waiting so long, that, with the end in sight, he may have looked to marry another, perhaps a foreign princess whose country would support him in his battle with Pope and Emperor. Perhaps Anne sought to conceive Henry's son, relying on his obsession with the royal succession to keep him true to her.

In fact, it was Anne's discovery, in mid-January 1533, that she was pregnant which precipitated her (secret) marriage to Henry. By Easter, Archbishop Cranmer had supplied the divorce, and Anne was at last proclaimed queen. At Whitsun she was crowned. In September she gave birth—to a daughter.

The speed with which King Henry tired of Queen Anne is remarkable. Perhaps he found her (who may well have been completely inexperienced sexually before she became his mistress) not what he had desired, not the exciting bed-mate which her sophistication in years of love-play had seemed to promise. The King continued to sleep with his new wife, to live with her quite blithely, but at the same time it was obvious that he would not scruple to take a mistress.

Through 1534 and 1535 Anne attempted to keep Henry's love by giving him a son. But by the autumn of 1534 she had had three miscarriages and was in low spirits: it was then that she heard that her husband was paying court to a lady (whose name is not recorded). In panic, she turned for help to her wily sister-in-law Jane, Lady Rochford, and together they set in train some plot (whose details have not survived) to oust her rival. It failed. The King learned of Queen Anne's machinations and was roused to fury. Lady Rochford was banished from Court.

Anne tried again. Early in 1535 she produced a cousin of her own, Madge Shelton, whom she hoped would attract Henry but who would be so grateful to Anne for her advancement

that she would do her no harm, while at the same time keeping
the King from more dangerous women. But Henry saw through
the ploy and sent Madge away. He took other mistresses, or so
it was said, but not the one offered by his wife.

The consolation of royal dignity, of leadership of the Court,
of command over unlimited jewels and robes, and of her infant
daughter, Elizabeth, on whom the King doted, may have kept
Anne Boleyn's courage up while she faced her problems. But
there was little encouragement from her husband's subjects, no
demonstration of their affection and admiration for her when
she appeared in public. England was already torn by the religious controversy which marred Henry VIII's reign, and men
were even then going to the gallows and the block for their
loyalty to papal authority: Anne was everywhere reviled as the
supplanter of the popular Queen Catherine, as the cause of
religious persecution. Her enemies labelled her 'the Concubine',
'the goggle-eyed whore'.

Occasionally the King and Queen quarrelled bitterly: it was
inevitable with Henry's temper and Anne's temperament, but
for the most part the couple appeared to be on amicable terms,
and 1535 went by untroubled by any repetition of Henry's
infidelities. In June Anne became pregnant again: her spirits
lifted and the King's hopes soared. In January 1536 Catherine
of Aragon, long since sent into prison in the country, died,
protesting to the last that she was Henry's legal, loving wife:
the King was upset on receiving her last letter, but both he and
Anne were relieved to be rid of her.

Henry celebrated the event by staging a tournament, in
which he himself took part in jousting contests. But here disaster struck. The King was thrown from his horse and for two
hours lay unconscious. When the news was brought to Anne,
she was horrified. She realised, maybe for the first time, that
if her husband died, England would be thrown into civil war
by the rival claims to the throne of her child and Catherine's,
and with her own unpopularity in the kingdom, she would be in
the utmost danger. It was enough to send Anne prematurely
into labour. She gave birth to a boy, but he was dead.

Queen Anne may also have realised, at this point, that
Queen Catherine's death was not a blessing to her but an added
hazard to her already precarious position. As long as Catherine
lived, Henry would not discard her (Anne) and take another

wife, for as long as his first queen lived there would always remain the doubt that the divorce was illegal and on the validity of any subsequent marriage. With Catherine dead, Henry was indubitably free to marry again.

Through the spring of 1536 Anne Boleyn recovered her strength but not her spirits. The King was paying court to one of her maids-of-honour, Jane Seymour; rumours were flying that Henry was planning another divorce; Anne's former friends and protégés were deserting her.

In fact, the King was planning more than a divorce, which, like the first, would be open to doubt without papal permission (which would obviously be neither sought nor offered). His loyal and obsequious councillor Thomas Cromwell was already gathering evidence which was intended to prove that Queen Anne had been flagrantly unfaithful to the King, that she merited death for her treason.

On the morning of 2 May 1536 a deputation of members of the Privy Council, including her own uncle the Duke of Norfolk, presented themselves to the Queen. They told her of the arrest of her alleged lovers and enumerated the charges against her: adultery, incest and intent to murder the King. Anne begged to be allowed to see her husband, but this was refused and she was ordered to prepare for her journey to the Tower.

The cases of the four supposed lovers were held first, at Westminster, and all but one fiercely rejected the charge. (It is possible that the odd man out, a Court musician named Mark Smeaton, was forced by torture to plead guilty.) But all were sentenced to death.

Similarly, at her trial in the Tower, Anne also pleaded not guilty to all the charges, and her brother, Lord Rochford, denied that he had ever slept with her. Anne spoke out bravely: she had never taken a lover, she said, never promised to marry any man with an eye to the King's death. But of course, no one chose to believe her or to take her part. And it was her uncle the Duke of Norfolk who passed the sentence.

Because thou hast offended our sovereign lord the King's Grace, in committing treason against his person, and art here attainted of the same, the law of the realm is this: that thou shalt be burned here, within the Tower of London, on the Green—else to have thy head smitten off, as the King's pleasure be further known of the same.[5]

The date of the Queen's execution (by the sword—so far was Henry merciful) was set for 17 May, but it was postponed for two days to allow arrangements to be made for the royal divorce. This was essential if Anne's daughter Elizabeth was to be removed from the royal succession. In fact, by this assertion that Henry and Anne had never been legally married (on the pretext of his former relations with her sister, which gave them the same degrees of relationship as a brother- and sister-in-law), the charge of adultery was negated, but this irony was ignored.

Shortly before noon on the morning of 19 May 1536, Queen Anne Boleyn mounted the scaffold which had been erected on Tower Green, lay her head on the block and offered her neck to the sword's sharp edge.

Even before Anne's death, Henry VIII had made clear his intention of marrying Jane Seymour, and the wedding took place on 30 May.

The new Queen was the daughter of a mere country gentleman, and was a pious and modest girl, more like the King's first wife than the fascinating Anne. Her virtue was undoubted, but, so cheap were the reputations of most Court ladies of the time that the imperial ambassador found it amazing: "You may imagine whether being an Englishwoman and having been long at Court, she would not hold it a sin to be a maid"[8]—but she was.

After the death of Jane Seymour in the autumn of 1537— the price of her gift to Henry of the longed-for son—the King continued his chequered matrimonial career, taking three more wives over the next decade; but he had no known mistress in these years.

Anne Boleyn's young cousin Catherine Howard might have become Henry's mistress, had she not had ambitious relations to ensure that the King married her. She arrived at Court in 1539, in her mid-teens, to be a maid-of-honour to Henry's fourth wife, Anne of Cleves, but had soon supplanted Anne, who suffered under the twin drawbacks, in the King's eyes, of plainness and Protestantism. In July 1540 Catherine Howard became Queen of England.

It might well be thought that Catherine should go down on her knees in gratitude to a kindly Providence which had so raised her, for all her life until now she had been a poor relation in the house of the Dowager Duchess of Norfolk, her step-grandmother, brought up by servants and usually ignored. And it would be reasonable to suppose that Catherine would profit by the example of her cousin Anne and become a faithful, docile wife. However, though the young Queen took as her motto the words "No wish save his", and though she never teased Henry with caprices as had Anne Boleyn, she was soon betraying her husband.

Catherine could not escape from her past. The favours which she now showered on her former companions take on a sinister complexion, a suggestion of her submission to blackmail, when one realises that the gentlewomen who came from the Duchess of Norfolk's household to serve the Queen knew all about Catherine's former *amours*.

Despite the old Duchess's strictness, her attendants had managed to enjoy themselves when their lady was safely asleep. After lights out, their sweethearts could creep into the young women's dormitory, there to enjoy midnight feasts, muffled carousals and other, less innocent, pastimes.

Catherine was only about fourteen years old when she took her first lover, one Henry Manox, son of a local squire, who was employed to teach her Howard cousins music. Catherine and Manox took to meeting secretly, trysting even in the Duchess's chapel chamber, a small sacristy behind the altar. The girl's grandmother seems to have known something of the *affaire*, but to have taken little account of it. However, when rumours started that Manox and Catherine were secretly engaged, one of the senior gentlewomen, Mary Lassells, took it upon herself to warn him that he was going too far. If the Duchess found out what was going on, declared Mistress Lassells, she would set some of her kin to kill him.

By then the household had left the Duchess's country mansion for Norfolk House, near Lambeth, and there, in contact with a wider world, Catherine gave Manox a rival. He was Francis Dereham, a handsome gentleman attendant on the Duke of Norfolk. Soon he was a regular visitor to the dormitory, a gracious bestower of sweetmeats and trinkets on the adoring Catherine. And in return he received more than kisses.

The idyll of young love ended in the autumn of 1539 when Catherine was sent to Court. But, significantly, she and Dereham were thrown together once more in August 1541, when he was appointed the Queen's secretary: in later days she would assert that she had taken him on at her step-grand-mother's request, so perhaps the Dowager Duchess too was now going in fear of past sins coming to light. But still, even with royal favour, Dereham could not be trusted to be discreet; he was even heard to remark that, were the King to die, the Queen would speedily marry him.

In fact, Catherine was no longer in love with Dereham. Soon after her wedding she had fallen under the spell of one of her maternal cousins, Thomas Culpeper, a gentleman of the King's Privy Chamber. There is nothing, however, to confirm the later traditions that the pair had known and loved each other since childhood: Catherine's alleged words on the block that she died the wife of the King but would rather have been the wife of Culpeper are certainly apocryphal.

By the spring of 1541 Catherine and Thomas were exchanging love-letters, and soon they were arranging secret meetings. Catherine's only confidante now was her cousin by marriage Jane, Viscountess Rochford (widow of Anne Boleyn's brother and alleged lover), and when the Court went 'on progress' to the north that summer, in every house at which the royal party stayed along the route, Lady Rochford would seek out means of bringing the Queen's lover secretly to her at night. Inevitably, the servants, especially those who knew Catherine of old, began to suspect the truth.

For a long time, the King did not. Still infatuated with Catherine, he was blind to all but his love for her.

It was the meddling Mary Lassells who started the ball rolling. She told her brother John (a fervent Protestant who loathed the Howards' pro-Catholic dominance in the Council) all she knew about the Queen's past. John Lassells went to Archbishop Cranmer, in duty bound, so he said, to apprise the King of his wife's infamy. Cranmer was a good man, incapable of self-interest at the expense of another but dominated by a powerful conscience, which told him that Henry should know all. It took much courage, however, for him to present the King with a letter detailing Catherine's early sexual exploits, which he did on 2 November 1541.

Henry would not believe it. The investigation which he ordered was intended to protect Catherine from slander, not to prove her guilt. But so thorough was the enquiry, so many were the witnesses called, so pertinent and so damning were their statements, that before the week was out, the King could be left in no doubt of his young wife's duplicity. If he told himself that "there was no fool worse than an old fool", he was not far wrong. On the evening of Sunday 6 November Henry left Hampton Court, where he and Catherine had been staying on their return from the north, leaving the Queen behind.

At first the investigators concentrated on trying to prove that Catherine had been 'pre-contracted'—that is betrothed—to Dereham, to bring her down with a charge of bigamy: then they uncovered evidence of her recent adultery and changed the charge to that of treason.

Once again, the Duke of Norfolk was called upon to prove his own fidelity to the Crown by confronting a niece with her crimes. He interviewed Catherine, with Cranmer, on 7 November. The girl broke down almost immediately, crying and confessing. She admitted, in recorded words whose confusion have a ring of authenticity, that Dereham had gone to bed with her "sometimes in his doublet and hose, and two or three times naked, but not so naked that he had nothing upon him, for he had always at least his doublet and, as I do think, his hose also, but I mean naked when his hose were put down".[7] She would not admit, however, that there had been any sort of marriage between them, not even the solemn betrothal which could be counted as a form of marriage in the sixteenth century. Nor, in later interviews, would she admit having committed adultery with Culpeper.

One by one Catherine's ladies were questioned, unable to say for certain that the Queen had been Culpeper's mistress, because she and Lady Rochford had been so careful to keep their secret. They could only voice their suspicions. Manox (perhaps under torture) admitted intimacy with Catherine short of intercourse; Dereham confessed all; Culpeper could be brought to say only that both he and Catherine had "intended and meant to do ill".

No time was wasted in bringing the guilty to account. Proceedings opened at Hampton Court on 22 November. On 1 December Dereham and Culpeper were tried at the Guildhall and convicted of treason: both were sentenced to be hanged, drawn and quartered; both petitioned the King to have the sentence commuted to that of beheading—only Culpeper was accorded that mercy.

Once again, the craven Duke of Norfolk saved himself by ranging himself among the prosecutors. He provided information against his stepmother: that she had broken into a chest which Dereham had left in her keeping and had destroyed certain letters. In the first week of December the Dowager Duchess and other members of the Howard family were brought into the Tower. They were tried on the 2nd: the Dowager first for her treason in destroying Dereham's probably treasonable letters, a charge then reduced to misprision of treason for having concealed her knowledge of Catherine's unchastity at the time of her wedding to the King; and with her Catherine's uncle William and his wife Margaret, her aunt Lady Bridgewater and her sister-in-law Anne, all for the same crime. All were found guilty, all sentenced to forfeiture of their possessions and perpetual imprisonment.

Lady Rochford, whose culpability was the greater, was to be tried with the Queen. They were to be arraigned under a bill of attainder, a method which denied them any defence and which offered only one penalty: death. Catherine's treason lay in her concealment of her "unchaste life" before her marriage, so that the King had taken her in the belief that she was "a pure and clean maiden", and her adultery, through which she might have tried to pass off another man's child as the King's.

Catherine was not present while Parliament debated her guilt (she was in custody at Sion House on the Thames near Brentford): the first reading of the bill took place on 21 January 1542; due form was observed, but by 11 February the death warrant had already been drawn up and was enacted. Lady Rochford too was condemned.

Catherine Howard had not the courage of her cousin Anne: perhaps her guilt was the greater—for it has never been unanimously agreed that the charges against Henry VIII's second wife were anything more than a pretext for her death, while the guilt of the fifth seems certain. Catherine alternated between moods of hysteria and calm, of disregard for her approaching death and then an obsession with the subject; sometimes she seemed cheerful, at others melancholy. But to the end she was considerate to her family, begging the King not to "impute her crime" to her kindred.

On 10 February Londoners might have seen a procession of boats coming from Sion to the Tower. But they were allowed no view of the Queen: her barge was enclosed.

On the 13th some few were allowed into the Tower precincts to stand with the dignitaries to witness the beheading of Queen Catherine Howard and Lady Rochford.

Henry VIII's career as a lover was over. He had been stunned by his fifth wife's conduct, was ageing and ill. By the time he married his sixth wife, the twice-widowed Catherine Parr, he was more in need of a nurse than a bed-companion.

For all the flamboyant reputation of Henry VIII, his fame as a lover rests almost entirely on his devotion to Anne Boleyn. For the most part his marriages were made for policy, to provide heirs to the throne, not for love or lust. His mistresses were few compared with the number kept by foreign monarchs. Nor did the moral climate in England at the time approximate that in, say, France: some of the nobility kept mistresses, but they were not flaunted and paraded as were their counterparts in France. The majority of English men and women in the reign of Henry VIII most strongly disapproved of the King's matrimonial adventures. Whatever the sexual morals of the populace, they would prefer a king and a queen of blameless life.

5

The Virgin Queen

In 1558 the Scottish Church-reformer John Knox published his
*First blast of the trumpet against the monstrous regiment of
women*, a vehement denunciation of government by queens. He
certainly had many targets for his venom, for there was an
unprecedented number of queens in power in Europe at the
time: France was ruled by a queen regent, Catherine de' Medici,
Scotland by another, Marie de Guise, and after her death in
1560, by her daughter the queen regnant Mary Stuart; until
1558 the ruler of England was Mary Tudor, Henry VIII's
daughter by Catherine of Aragon, who was succeeded by her
half-sister, Anne Boleyn's daughter Elizabeth.

Of course, John Knox was not to know that Elizabeth I
would reign gloriously over England for more than forty years,
and that her reign would be acknowledged as a golden age in
the nation's history. In 1558, many, like Knox, could point to
the dangers inherent in rule by queens.

One of them was the problem of woman's inadequacy for the
task—or so it seemed to contemporaries. In fact, the women of
the sixteenth century were far from being the demure and silent,
timid and ignorant creatures of popular legend: working-class
women were as firmly as ever bound to the toil of house and
farm, but in the middle classes there were women running
businesses, trading on their own account and administering
substantial sums of money, while aristocratic ladies often governed immense estates, commanded hundreds of servants and
labourers and still found time to engage in cultural and intellec-
tual pursuits: these great ladies were often as well educated as
their husbands and brothers, highly respected by scholars and
churchmen. But still, in theory, women were subservient to
men: the letters of St. Paul were still quoted to show that
women must obey the men whom God had ordained to be their
masters. In such a climate, therefore, a woman to whom chance

or Providence gave a crown was in a difficult position: it was taken for granted that she must seek a husband to rule on her behalf.

But this raised a second problem. Where a country lived under a queen regnant, there was always the danger that she would marry a foreign prince who would bring his wife's subjects under the power of his own government. Mary Tudor had thrown herself joyfully into the arms of her young Spanish bridegroom, the Emperor's son Philip, and happily embraced the imperial, and Catholic, influence which he imposed on her regime. It was largely imperial pressure which had induced Mary to persecute her Protestant subjects, for at the outset of her reign, before the Emperor and his son made their influence felt, she had been notably merciful.

Mary, Queen of Scots, was even then controlled by France, whose King François II was her first husband, and whose leading peers, the Guise family, were her close kin. France sent troops and counsellors to Scotland to support her mother's Catholic policies against the Calvinism of the majority of Scotsmen.

Just as dangerous, however, was a queen's marriage to one of her own subjects. The power of one noble family and its supporters would alienate rival nobles from the throne, and could lead to civil war. In the 1560s, Mary Stuart's second husband, Lord Darnley, built up his own party within the Scottish government, attempting to rule through his wife for his own aggrandisement and the furtherance of his own policies; her third husband, the Earl of Bothwell, was another faction-monger, and the outcry against his potential rule drove his rivals into revolt with disastrous consequences for the Queen.

However, Elizabeth Tudor came to the throne with a full awareness of her problems, and approached them more cautiously than did her sister and her cousin. She fully recognised the dangers of committing herself, by marriage, to any foreign power, and took great pains to prevent factionalism within her own government. Nor would she allow her own power to be set at naught but determined always to be the real fount of government in England. In the reigns of her father, brother and sister, she had been a pawn in the game of politicians, with no control over her own fate: never again would she allow any man or party to rule her life.

But there were personal reasons too, deep, maybe subconscious fears which prevented Elizabeth's marrying. She had her father's marital career before her: who could blame her if she associated matrimony with death, with her own mother and her aunt/stepmother brought to the block by offending the King? From this premise, many psychologist biographers have suggested that one reason for Elizabeth's cherished reputation as 'the virgin queen' may well have been her deep-rooted fear of marriage. The Queen may, as she is alleged to have once confessed, have had some deformity of her sexual organs—more likely the deformity was in her mind, which repulsed the thought of marriage even while she seemed outwardly to desire it. All this apart, a sentimentalist would say, more simply, that she desired to be loved for herself, not for her crown and power, and that her rank made this impossible.

Elizabeth had learned early in life what it was to be courted by a man seeking power through her. During the reign of her half-brother Edward VI, his Seymour uncles had been foremost in royal government: one, the Duke of Somerset, as the boy-King's Lord Protector, another, Thomas, as Lord High Admiral. But Thomas was jealous of his brother's greater title, and, having failed to achieve parity by marrying Henry VIII's widow and by winning the affection of young Edward, sought other means to further his ambition.

Even in Queen Catherine Parr's lifetime, Seymour was pursuing their ward, Princess Elizabeth, with an eye to taking the throne, as her husband, at some future date. In her early teens, Elizabeth was a precociously attractive, sensual girl, with all the verve of her Tudor-Boleyn blood, and she was by no means averse either to flattery, such as Seymour lavished on her, or to sexual games: the Lord Admiral would come upon her in her bed in the mornings and tickle her until she screamed for mercy; he would romp with her in the gardens, even under his wife's eye.

Lord Protector Somerset realised the extent of his brother's ambitions. After the death of Catherine in 1548, it became obvious that Lord Thomas was angling to make Elizabeth his wife; at the same time, he was hedging his bets by taking on the guardianship of a Tudor cousin, Lady Jane Grey, who, once married to the King, could further his influence in royal government—or, if Elizabeth's claim to the throne and that of her half-sister Mary, were set aside, Jane's Tudor ancestry would make her a feasible candidate as Edward VI's successor. Either way, the child was a useful pawn to Lord Thomas. But the plans involving Elizabeth and Jane were long-term projects, and by the end of 1548 Seymour could wait no longer to supplant his brother. In January 1549 he made an attempt to kidnap the King.

Now Somerset struck. He had Lord Thomas arrested, charged with treason and hurried to the block.

At the time, it was widely rumoured that the Princess Elizabeth was pregnant by Seymour, which her enforced absence from Court after the death of her supposed lover seemed to confirm. The sixteen-year-old Elizabeth might reasonably have quaked at such a scandal, might have panicked and made mistakes: in fact, she was prematurely wise, with the guile of self-protection and an instinct for survival. Defending herself by attacking (a trick which was to serve her well all her life), she wrote at once to Protector Somerset demanding a public denial of these rumours, "to send a proclamation into the countries [that is, counties] that they refrain their tongues, declaring how the tales be but lies, it should make the people think that you and the Council have great regard that no such rumours should be spread of any of the King's Majesty's sisters".[1] Elizabeth won her point. But whether she had had tender feelings for Thomas Seymour, what his death cost her, no one can know.

Over the next years the Princess became adept at fending off such attacks as that of 1549. During the reign of her half-sister Mary, she was more than once suspected of conspiring to take the throne, more than once put into confinement—even in the Tower. But she survived, to become queen in November 1558.

From the outset of her reign, Queen Elizabeth I received petitions from her loyal Parliament that she should marry and provide heirs to the throne. At the same time, there was no dearth of foreign princes willing to become the English queen's consort and to gain an alliance for their homeland. From Scandinavia, from the German states, from France—even from Spain, where Elizabeth's brother-in-law King Philip II declared love for her, there poured in proposals of marriage.

The Queen could not afford to offend her neighbours or her subjects, so she answered courteously and tactfully all representations made to her on the subject of marriage, but neither then nor later would she allow herself to be persuaded or bludgeoned into taking a husband.

By as early a date as 1559, there seemed to be one favourite in the race towards the royal altar and throne. This was Lord Robert Dudley, survivor of his family's fall after their attempt of 1553 to put Lady Jane Grey on the throne. By his own assertion, he had known Elizabeth intimately since childhood (they were, apparently, of equal age, born on the same day in September 1533), and during Mary's reign they had been prisoners in the Tower at the same time—though there is no evidence to show that they were permitted to meet there: certainly, Dudley had been in the inner circle around the royal family for many years, no stranger to Elizabeth, and in the months after her accession he was the man closest to her, apparently the man most likely to marry her.

However, he already had a wife, Amy Robsart, whom he had married several years earlier. The couple had been matched, as was usual at the time, to serve their parents' ends: Amy's inheritance matched Robert Dudley's rank very suitably, and there is no evidence to suggest that they loved each other. She lived in the country, taking no part in Dudley's Court career and seemingly visited by him only occasionally.

In April 1559 the Spanish ambassador reported to his king that, "During the last few days, Lord Robert has come so much into favour that he does what he likes with affairs, and it is even said that Her Majesty visits him in his chamber day and night. People talk so freely of this that they go so far as to say that his wife has a malady in one of her breasts and the Queen is only waiting for her to die to marry Lord Robert." Ambassador de Feria added that, "Sometimes [Elizabeth] speaks like a woman who will only accept a great prince, and then they say she is in love with Lord Robert and will never let him leave her."[2]

Then, suddenly, on the evening of 8 September 1560, Amy Dudley was found lying dead at the foot of a staircase at her house, Cumnor Place, in Berkshire. Within days, rumours were circulating through England and soon on the Continent that she had been murdered at Dudley's order—even with the Queen's knowledge or connivance. A hastily-summoned coroner's jury gave a verdict of accidental death, but there still seemed no good reason for her fall, and for years afterwards the widower was under suspicion.

Only in the past twenty years has modern medicine discovered that cancer of the breast, such as Amy Dudley suffered, may cause a spontaneous fracture of the spine at the neck.

The death of Amy Dudley cast a blight on Elizabeth's spirits and on Dudley's advancement. He had expected to be created a duke, but he was not, and the Queen's former generosity to him in lands and appointments and money was for a time curtailed. But it was a long time before suspicion of murder was allowed to lapse, and had Elizabeth married Dudley then or later, it would surely have revived. Lord Robert went on hoping, however, canvassing support in the royal Council and even for the approval of the King of Spain: for years he seems to have had firm expectations of becoming Elizabeth's husband, but the marriage never transpired. The Queen continued to keep him close to her, showing him affection in public, and renewed her gifts to him, including an earldom (of Leicester, in 1564), but there is no evidence that she ever thought to marry him.

Nor is there evidence that Elizabeth and Robert Dudley were lovers, though there were occasional rumours to that effect. In October 1564, she told the Spanish ambassador that,

I am insulted both in England and abroad, for having shown too much favour to the Lord Robert. I am spoken of as if I were an immodest woman. I ought not to wonder at it: I have favoured him because of his excellent disposition and his many merits, but I am young and he is young, and therefore we have both been slandered. God knows they do us grievous wrong, and the time will come when the world will know it also. A thousand eyes see all that I do, and calumny will not fasten on me for ever.[3]

If Dudley—her contemporary, her intimate companion, her obvious favourite for so many years—was not Elizabeth's lover, then surely no man was. There were, as we shall see, numerous rivals for her affection and more tangible rewards, but not one with so strong a pull on her heart-strings.

Public opinion would scarcely have tolerated a promiscuous queen. Two centuries later, Elizabeth of Russia, secure in her autocracy, could take innumerable lovers with impunity, but Elizabeth of England always recognised that her safety and her tenure of the throne depended to a great extent on the personal loyalty of her subjects: she, Head of the Church of

England, could not flout God's laws and her people's code of morals.

However, where no man was the Queen's lover, every man was—or was expected to be. Short of physical surrender and emotional dependence, Elizabeth thoroughly enjoyed the game of love. Throughout her long reign, even after she had lost those attractions of face and figure which she had vaunted in her youth, the Queen kept up the charade that she was the most beautiful, most desirable woman in her kingdom; and her wise courtiers, who knew how generous she could be to those who pleased her, kept up the pretence too. In part, of course, this was a shrewd ploy of Elizabeth's: to establish a convention of intense loyalty to herself, which could be used for practical purposes in politics—but the love-cravings of her ego should not be ignored.

Elizabeth surrounded herself with a brilliant Court, which, almost every summer, she took into the countryside, drawing crowds of gaping subjects to gaze at, and remember all their lives, their fairy-tale Queen. She lived amid a continual pageant, herself the star of the show. In their verses Court poets hailed her as 'Gloriana', 'Belphoebe', 'Astraea' and so on, likening her to classical goddesses and mythical queens of antiquity and romance, and employing the most fervent language in her praise. Spenser's epic *The Faerie Queen*, with its florid verbiage and striking story-lines, was the epitome and masterpiece of the genre.

In Elizabeth's youth, maturity and old age, a stream of men gave her the devotion she craved, providing Dudley with rivals to annoy and worry him and to intensify his attentions to the Queen.

One of the many young hopefuls who presented themselves at Court soon after Elizabeth's accession, flattering, fawning and picking up what offices and perquisites they could, was Sir William Pickering. He came with a great reputation as a womaniser, with good looks and charm of manner and a polish acquired at the French Court: but his reign lasted only a short time, for his pride in royal favour had made him overbearing among the other courtiers, and, once his novelty had worn off, Elizabeth had no use for him.

Christopher Hatton lasted longer. He was a young lawyer from Northampton, so tall and handsome that the Queen made

Robert Devereux, second Earl of Essex: more than thirty years his senior, Elizabeth I was flattered by his devotion—then shattered by his betrayal of her trust.

Robert Dudley, Earl of Leicester: the acknowledged favourite of Elizabeth I in the early years of her reign, he constantly intrigued to marry her.

George Villiers, Duke of Buckingham: the most powerful of royal paramours, through the influence he exerted on the besotted James I.

Robert Carr, Earl of Somerset: one of the homosexual lovers of James I—his career ended in 1618 after his implication in a murder case.

him the leader of her hand-picked band of gentlemen pensioners. When, in 1575, Hatton went abroad to find health at a spa, he wrote to the Queen with as much passion as ever Henry VIII had addressed to Anne Boleyn:

My spirit and soul, I feel, agreeth with my body and life, that to serve you is a heaven; but to lack you is more than hell's torment unto them. . . . Would God I were with you but for one hour! . . . Bear with me, my dear sweet lady: passion overcometh me. . . . Love me, for I love you. . . . Your bondsman, everlastingly tied,

Christopher Hatton.[4]

But he was no mere lap-dog: Hatton served on royal commissions, sat in Parliament, dispensed justice and was a fine administrator. At length he became Lord Chancellor.

Among the many others was Thomas Heneage, gentleman of the Queen's Privy Chamber, Treasurer of her household, then, in succession to Hatton, her Vice-Chamberlain. There was also the young Edward Vere, Earl of Oxford: when he came home from Italy after a brief holiday, he was laden with gifts for the Queen. Later he marred his own career, which had started so promisingly, by turning Catholic, pursuing, seemingly indiscriminately, Elizabeth's maids-of-honour and brawling around the town.

The Queen hated to see any of her favourites marry—a 'dog in the manger' attitude. Walter Raleigh might have won an earldom or estates, or at least something more than a cell in the Tower, had he not seduced the maid-of-honour Elizabeth Throckmorton. He had the great advantage of being a nephew of Elizabeth's former governess, Kate Ashley, who had gone through all the hard times with her and who remained a royal confidante until her, Kate's, death. Even without Mistress Ashley's patronage, however, Raleigh was just such a man as the Queen most admired, dashing and courageous, enterprising and ambitious, cultured and eloquent, but he had just too much eccentric independence to knuckle under Elizabeth's possessive tyranny.

That she was possessive cannot be denied. And if one of the second rank of her favourites such as Raleigh could incur such wrath by marrying, how much worse was it when the Queen discovered Dudley's infidelity.

It was during Hatton's heyday that Dudley (now Earl of Leicester) began toying with various Court ladies—probably at first to make Elizabeth jealous and turn her from Hatton. One of them, the widowed Lady Douglas Sheffield (née Howard, a cousin of the Queen) became his mistress in about 1570 and presented him with a son and namesake in August 1574. It is likely that Elizabeth knew of her favourite's lapse, for she was seen to be ill-disposed to Lady Sheffield, but nothing was said at the time. But that *affaire* dwindled, and within a couple of years the Earl was entangled with another royal cousin, Lettice, Countess of Essex (née Knollys, a granddaughter of Elizabeth's aunt Mary Boleyn and remarkably resembling the Queen in looks). The couple married secretly in 1578—only weeks before the birth of their child.

Even then, Leicester did not confess to the Queen. It was only in August 1579 that one Jean Simier, a Frenchman in the service of the Duke of Alençon, informed Elizabeth of her favourite's duplicity. But then Simier had good reason for doing so: he was preparing the way for his master to woo the Queen, and was glad to find a means of discrediting Leicester, the main stumbling-block—or so it seemed—to a royal marriage.

The tempers of the Tudor family were notorious. They raged; they shouted; they swore. But what Henry VIII had fired at the ministers and wives who flouted him was nothing compared with the vituperations which Elizabeth I screamed when she heard of Leicester's treachery. She was barely stopped from sending him to the Tower, and for some time he skulked timorously on the fringes of Court and capital, not daring to approach her.

In her malevolence, the Queen attempted to break the marriage. Lady Sheffield had once tried to prove that she had been married to Leicester, asserting that they had gone through a ceremony of affirmation before witnesses back in 1571; since then, she had given up her suit and had married Sir Edward Stafford, but now she was brought before royal Councillors and required to tell them all about that contract with Leicester: Elizabeth swore that, if that earlier wedding could be proved valid, the Earl must give up Lettice and acknowledge Douglas as his wife. In fact, Lady Stafford had no wish to leave her new husband for the man who had cast her off: she provided no concrete proof that she was the true Countess of

Leicester. So Lettice was vindicated, and the marriage had to stand.

But Elizabeth could not long deny herself the pleasure of Robert Dudley's company. He was back at Court to see her being wooed by François of Alençon that summer, to see her nursing the Duke through illness with her own hands, and to hear her calling him her pet 'frog', though she never came to the point of accepting the Frenchman's proposals of marriage. By the end of 1579, Leicester was back in his old position of trust about the Queen, careful to keep his wife beyond the range of Elizabeth's spiteful glares.

The Queen kept up the pretence of considering the Duke of Alençon's suit for many years, largely, it seems, as a means of quieting the ever-increasing demands that she should marry. While she had a suitor at hand, she could appear to be prepared to marry; by this temporising she offended no one and kept her independence. But her ministers fumed at the delays, anxious that the Queen should produce an heir to the throne. An alternative to marriage, they argued, would be for her to name an heir from among her relations, and then she would be free to marry or not as she pleased. Elizabeth would not, however, agree to this either. Whatever her objections to matrimony, she had good reason to fear an heir named in her own lifetime; had she not herself, as heir to her half-sister, become a focal point for all dissidents from Mary's government? She could envisage a time when her own heir would build up a party against her, Elizabeth's, interests. With an ambitious, impatient heir, she would be forever looking over her shoulder, fearing opposition to every unpopular policy, wary even of assassination to make way for the new monarch. In the 1580s, Elizabeth faced, dealt with and overcame the pretensions to her throne of both Mary, Queen of Scots, and Philip of Spain, and, to the last moments of her life, she managed to stave off her ministers' demands that the succession question be resolved. It was a masterly vindication of her policy that she avoided all the perils inherent in her situation.

In fact, Elizabeth was remarkably successful in all she undertook, proving a woman's competence to rule as well as reign. Faced with complex problems in government, diplomacy and religion, she kept a balance between all shades of opinion and between rival parties in Council.

Only in the last years of her long life did Elizabeth Tudor begin to fail, to see the framework of her regime begin to crumble as Parliament sought to take on the powers which had formerly been the prerogative of royal government. At the same time, her control over her personal life weakened, and for the first time the Queen almost came to disaster through her favours to one of her 'lovers'.

The Earl of Leicester had died in 1588, clouding Elizabeth's pleasure in her navy's victory over the Spanish Armada : long since accepted back into her affections, he had proved his worth time and again in Council and, more recently, in war, and his death came as a blow after thirty years of intimacy. But even before Leicester's death, another man had come to take possession of the Queen's heart. In fact, he was Leicester's own stepson, son of his wife Lettice : Robert Devereux, Earl of Essex, by a quarter of a century Elizabeth's junior.

Essex was undeniably an attractive young man, with a flair and panache which put his rivals in the shade, but he was wily and selfish, self-centred and possessed of an ambition tinged by madness.

To all but Elizabeth herself, the Earl's professions of devotion must have sounded hollow. He had never seen her in the days when she had been vibrant and attractive, lithe and graceful : now the Queen was ageing fast, her face painted in a ghastly white mask in an attempt to bring back the glowing complexion of her youth, her thinning hair covered with a bright red wig, her dignity undiminished but shored up with the voluminous skirts, huge ruffs and brilliant jewels which gave her such distinction. Essex could not remember Elizabeth in the days when her affections might be valued on their own merit, as the favour of a radiantly attractive woman : now she was merely an elderly dotard dispensing power and titles and wealth on gigolos.

The Queen certainly doted on the Earl of Essex. Time and again she forgave his petty treacheries and insolence. She forgave him when, twice, he challenged rivals to a duel; she forgave him when he flirted with her maids-of-honour, girls young enough to be her granddaughters; she forgave him his run-away marriage—and his run-away attempt to join her armies abroad without her permission.

But she could not forgive Essex his more dangerous treachery of 1599, when he was—justifiably—suspected of plotting sedition in Ireland.

When the Earl heard that his enemies were using this fool-hardy venture to bring him down, he hastened home to England, relying on his formerly infallible charm to save himself. But it was too late. Elizabeth saved her dignity—and perhaps her throne—by admitting to herself and to her Councillors that Essex had gone too far. Even then he was spared a state trial on charges of treason and only censured by the private session of justice at which he appeared—so far did the Queen's mercy extend. Indeed, with caution and discretion Essex might in time have retrieved his position.

But he was in the grip of a madness in which discretion, prudence and patience had no place.

With a small band of friends, the Earl formulated a wild plan: to take the Tower by storm, to raise support in the City of London, to march on the Court and take possession of the Queen, who was to be forced to make him Lord Protector of her realm. Under the guise of ridding Elizabeth of unworthy councillors, Essex would strike at his enemies and take control of the government.

On Sunday 8 February 1601 the Earl of Essex and his friends rode into London, trying to raise the citizens to their cause. But even as they did so, the barricades were going up outside the Palace of Whitehall and a force was being despatched to bring in this man who was now openly proclaimed a traitor.

Seeing his plans going awry, Essex retreated into his London mansion, intent on a foolhardy last stand. But the forces gathered round the area were too great to be fought by his small party, and surrender came before nightfall.

This time Essex was brought to trial, and now he was convicted of high treason and sentenced to death.

Even now, legend has it, the Earl might have saved himself. He had a ring which the Queen had once given him, the production of which would ensure him pardon for any crime. Now Essex sent the ring to Elizabeth, expecting to redeem that promise given in a moment of love. But it never reached her: it fell into the hands of Lady Nottingham, whose husband was one of Essex's enemies, and she held it back until after the Earl had been beheaded, on 25 February 1601. The tale may well be apocryphal, but it is certainly characteristic of those involved.

After Essex's death, Elizabeth began to shrivel, both physically and emotionally. All round her the men and women whom she had known from childhood were dying off, and their grandchildren were arriving at Court, while she, who might now have been a grandmother herself, was still childless and ever more alone.

On her deathbed, in March 1603, Queen Elizabeth I came to terms with her mortality and named her cousin James VI, King of Scotland as heir to her throne. Then, at about 3 a.m. on the morning of Thursday, 24 March 1603, she died.

Later, a small casket which the Queen had always kept by her bed was opened and its contents examined. It contained a parchment inscribed "His last letter", the last message she had received from Robert Dudley, Earl of Leicester, written shortly before his death in 1588. Of all the men who had loved her and who had pretended to, Leicester was the one who had most strongly affected the heart of 'the virgin queen'.

6

Steenie

In Scotland, until the sixteenth century, there had been no royal paramour, male or female, to rival the reputation or the powers of such as Alice Perrers and Piers Gaveston in England. Royal mistresses there were—in plenty—but their influence and rewards were apparently comparatively negligible.

For the most part, Scotland's kings took their mistresses from among the great families of the realm, and, in turn, their bastards married back into the nobility. Gordon, Hamilton, Elphinstone, Carmichael: scarcely a family in the peerage had not provided a royal bed-fellow or accepted a semi-royal bride. But while the mistresses played minor roles in royal life, the bastards did not: in Church and State they were among the foremost councillors and servants of their royal fathers and half-brothers. The most powerful and famous of them all was James Stewart, Earl of Moray, son of King James V and half-brother of Mary, Queen of Scots: first acting as Mary's chief councillor, after her deposition in 1567 Moray returned as Regent of the kingdom, giving Scotland its first period of peace in many a year, until he was murdered in 1570.

Mary Stuart's son King James VI of Scotland, a mere infant when the crown was thrust upon him, was not the ladies' man his grandfather and their forebears had been. For some reason, probably more emotional than physical, he was homosexual.

Historians have never satisfactorily assessed James's sexuality. Some have named each of his favourites as his lovers: others have queried whether the sexual act played any part in any of his relationships with other men; some say that one was a lover, another was not—rarely agreeing. Some stress James's fascination with male beauty, others his fatherliness to pretty young men.

Some historians have sought reasons for the King's homosexuality in his childhood, arguing that his enigmatic attitude to his mother—alleged murderess of his father, deserter of himself and traitor to her kingdom—formed the basis of his estrangement from all women. Some assert that his beautiful young wife, Anne of Denmark (whom he married in 1589), might have changed James's tastes had she made more intelligent use of her opportunities: for the first six months after their wedding, James was passionately attached to Anne, but then his interest dwindled, he returned to his minions and for the rest of their married life paid her little more than affectionately polite attention. As with many other homosexual kings, James did his duty in providing heirs to his throne (two sons and a daughter survived childhood), and the royal children made a bond between him and Anne rivalled only by that they shared in the hunting-field.

James adored his children, especially his only surviving daughter Elizabeth. In fact, he was at his best with those younger than himself, and with his dependents. He never grudged a wife to any of his young men, but adopted the brides as his daughters and frequently dandled their children. And it is a fascinating, surely unique phenomenon, that the King not only countenanced the friendship of his own last lover with his son Charles, but actually promoted it and showed not one sign of jealousy.

The first probable homosexual partner of James was his distant cousin Esmé Stuart, whom he created Earl then Duke of Lennox. Stuart came into James's life at an opportune moment: when the thirteen-year-old King was being stifled by factious counsellors and dour churchmen, the thirty-year-old Stuart arrived from France (in 1579), dazzling the boy with his sophistication, broad-minded approach to politics, casualness in religion and personal devotion to James himself. This in itself was enough to create hero-worship; Stuart's affectionate attentions to James, with an eye to furthering his own ambitions in politics, made the boy his slave. The riotous, loose-living courtiers brought to Scotland by Esmé Stuart (who taught James to swear and make bawdy jokes—a taste which never left him) had the easy morals of the Valois Court of France, where a flagrantly homosexual, king, Henri III, was then reigning: James's later Court was usually more circumspect, though contemporaries were frequently appalled by the drunkenness which was a habitual sight.

From childhood, James had seen little of women, and in his adolescence it was easier for him to form relationships with men of his own age than with girls: his chaplains, Presbyterian and strict, would have allowed short shrift to the King's dalliance with nubile young women, while young men were James's natural companions. By the time his governors realised the King's propensities and began to frown at his fawning on his minions, the royal favourites were already too powerful a band of lordlings to be ousted by royal servants.

From first to last, the majority of James's favourites were primarily interested in gaining political ascendancy over the King. Esmé Stuart certainly had pretensions to ruling through James: he arrived in Scotland in 1579 with the definite aim of re-establishing French influence in the kingdom and probably with some notion of re-establishing the Catholic Church there, or at least of gaining more toleration for his co-religionists. At the outset Lennox had to contend with the powers of the then Regent, the Earl of Morton (who had been foolishly weak in allowing this man, an obvious potential rival, to land in Scotland in the first place), but Morton was soon swept away: on the last day of December 1580 he was denounced as a conniver at the murder of James's father, back in 1566, and six months later went to the block.

For twenty months after Morton's fall, Lennox reigned supreme, having James's entire trust and confidence and holding the reins of government. What his plans were exactly, remains obscure: he had dealings with James's exiled mother (imprisoned in England), but he did not wholeheartedly support the projected Articles of Association which aimed to bring her back as co-ruler with her son. In any event, before Lennox could show his hand, before he could effect any real return to the French sphere of influence, his enemies banded against him. In August 1582 the 'Protestant lords' kidnapped the King, and by the end of the year Lennox had found it necessary, to save his life, to flee abroad. He never returned. James never saw him again.

As a young man in Scotland, the King continued to favour former friends of Lennox, and their politics. Patrick, Master of Gray, who had come with Lennox from France in 1579, was another of the alleged lovers of the King, an idle, extravagant man, who toyed with the dangerous game of corresponding with Mary, Queen of Scots.

More important, however, was George Gordon, Earl of Huntly, a Catholic (who intermittently pretended interest in conversion to the Protestant Church to please James) and leader of the Catholic lords in Council. Even when it was proved to the King that Huntly and his fellows had been in potentially treasonable correspondence with Philip of Spain, congratulating him in 1588 on his daring to flout English naval power, James remained loyal to his friend.

But even then events were brewing which would soon make King James of Scotland seriously ask himself who his friends were and how far they were to be trusted.

One of the foremost fermenters of trouble in these years was Francis Stewart, Earl of Bothwell (nephew and eventual heir of Mary Stuart's third husband). In the early 1580s the Earl had been one of the King's intimate circle, and James had been seen to "hang about his neck" and embrace him frequently in public, but before the decade ended, this love turned to the deepest fear and hatred. In part, James's mistrust of Bothwell was based on the fact that the Earl was a grandson of James's own grandfather James V, the son of one of that king's many bastards, and as such a feasible claimant to be James VI's heir until the birth of his own son in 1594. And Bothwell did nothing to dispel the King's fears: he made a pact with the Kirk which ranged him with James's political and religious critics; and he was said to be dabbling in witchcraft which, to the King's always superstitious mind, was a matter for horror. In fact, in 1591 Bothwell was charged with this crime by the 'proven' witches of North Berwick, who alleged that he had consulted them as to the date of the King's death and how it could be best accomplished.

From this point, the Earl of Bothwell was a virtual outlaw, though he still hoped to regain former royal favour and oust his enemies—most notably James's chief minister, Maitland—from control of the government. To this end he made three attempts to capture the King, failing each time but succeeding in terrifying James (whose turbulent childhood had taught him to fear the Scottish factionalism which made possession of his person a key factor in tenure of power).

At first, Huntly was James's firm supporter against Bothwell, but in February 1592, soon after their enemy's second attack, Huntly was closely implicated in the murder of a young Protestant politician, the Earl of Moray, and so fearful was he of prosecution by his personal enemies in the Kirk that in the summer of 1594 Huntly joined forces with Bothwell. However, the alliance had little effect: soon afterwards, faced with the Protestant loyalists in arms against them, both men fled abroad. Bothwell never dared return to Scotland, but Huntly made his submission to King and Kirk in 1597 and was not only restored in James's affections but was promoted to the title of marquis.

Throughout these years, as from childhood, the King lived in the midst of political intrigues, never knowing who was his disinterested friend, who his manipulator, who his enemy, who his potential assassin. In politics he acquired a devious guile which coloured his reign both in Scotland and, later, in England. Yet in his personal relationships he was trusting and loyal. It was a curious mixture which did not make for a stable character.

Always James looked forward to the day when he should be called to England to succeed Elizabeth I on the throne there. He tried to keep on good terms with his elderly, never-seen cousin—albeit insisting on complete freedom in Scottish affairs. Then, in the last years of the Queen's life, he was approached by her chief minister, Robert Cecil, and between them the two men laid plans for the peaceful transfer of power at Elizabeth's death. It is surely no coincidence that Cecil chose as his intermediary in the negotiations with James (and, perhaps, as the 'fall guy' if the dangerous correspondence was discovered) Lord Henry Howard, himself an alleged homosexual.

James was in his mid-thirties when, in March 1603, he fell heir to the English crown, and by now his tastes for bright and pretty young men had been firmly established. The current favourite, when the new King came south, was one James Hay, a smooth-faced, smooth-tongued young man who, as Master of the royal Wardrobe, was foremost of the Scots who spent prodigiously from their master's new treasury. But very soon Hay had a rival: Philip Herbert, scion of a noble House and proficient in the arts of hunting which James so admired. Herbert (whom the King created Earl of Montgomery) had little of the polish, elegance and chic of the general run of royal favourites, but he too had his day and his rewards. Like Hay, he was married off to a daughter of the English peerage, with the King hovering over his wedding as presiding deity, making broad jokes and winking: he appeared in Herbert's bedchamber on the morning after the wedding, still in his nightshirt, and an observer could not decide whether he sat upon or in the marriage-bed.

Since Huntly there had been no real political influence on James from his closest circle of intimates, and when he came to England, the King relied for the most part on the governmental expertise of Robert Cecil, who had allied with the Howard family to gain hegemony of Court and Council. But Cecil died in 1612, and the Howard triumvirate (the Earls of Northampton—the former Lord Henry, Suffolk and Nottingham) had not the same grip on affairs. It was then that James began to groom his new favourite, Robert Carr, Viscount Rochester, for power.

Carr had been several years in royal service before the King noticed him. Indeed, some years before, he had been dismissed for his *gaucherie* in service. Then, one day in 1607, when he was a page in the train of James Hay, Lord Doncaster, he attended his master at a tournament bearing Hay's ceremonial shield and had the good fortune to fall from his horse in full view of King James. Carr's fall brought about his rise: so struck was James by this lithe young man with bright yellow hair that he himself superintended the nursing of his broken bones. Thereafter the two were inseparable.

The Prince [that is, James—wrote a courtier] leaneth on his arm, pinches his cheek, smooths his ruffled garment, and, when he looketh on Carr, directeth discourse to divers others. This young man doth much study all art and device; he hath changed his tailors and tiremen many times, and all to please the Prince, who laugheth at the long grown fashion of our young courtiers and wisheth for change every day.

Carr hath all favours; the King teacheth him Latin every morning, and I think someone should teach him English too, for as he is a Scottish lad, he hath much need of better language. The King doth much covet his presence, the ladies too are not behindhand in their admiration; for I tell you this fellow is straight-limbed, well-favoured, strong-shouldered, and smooth-faced, with some sort of cunning and show of modesty; though, God wot, he well knoweth when to show his impudence.[1]

As well as attempting to teach Carr Latin, which proved a hopeless task, James introduced him to statecraft, intending that the young man should serve as his private secretary. Another mentor of Carr's was one Thomas Overbury, an old friend who pretended to great wisdom but who was rather out of his depth among the wily courtiers. At first James countenanced Overbury's tutelage of his own protégé and awarded him a knighthood; later, he became jealous.

After the death of Cecil, the Howard family lived in fear that the influence of their own 'Spanish party' might be overset by Carr's alliance with the 'Protestant party' in Council. The King prided himself on the peaceful years which his reign had initiated in England and on the understanding to which he had come with the kingdom's old enemy Spain in 1604, but there were men about him who intended to bring England back to a firmly Protestant stance in European diplomacy. Carr might have decided either way, according to where he might reap the best reward, were it not for his infatuation with a member of the Howard family, Frances, Countess of Essex, who won his allegiance for her kinsmen.

Frances, born in 1591, was a brightly-flowering teenager, married since 1606 to the young Earl of Essex. But Essex had spent the years since his wedding away on the Grand Tour, and in his absence his wife and Carr fell in love. Despite the Earl's protests, when he returned to claim his bride in 1610, Frances refused to cohabit with her husband and, it seems, evaded his sexual advances by debilitating him with potions which she obtained from the 'magician' Simon Forman.

In response to Carr's fervent pleas to have Frances as his wife, the King agreed to favour the annulment of marriage with Essex and even connived at having a commission pronounce judgment in her favour: when some of its members refused to return an obedient verdict, James appointed others, more complaisant, to provide the necessary votes. In December 1613, Frances Howard married Robert Carr: the King gave the bride £10,000 worth of jewels; the bridegroom he created Earl of Somerset.

Carr's old friend Overbury had at first approved his liaison with Lady Essex, and had even written the suitor's love-letters for him, but he could not approve the intended political alliance with the Howards. Soon Overbury began to make himself objectionable to Carr, who persuaded King James to offer his friend a foreign diplomatic appointment to remove him from the scene—only to have the offer rebuffed by Overbury. For his temerity, the unfortunate man was sent to the Tower. On 14 September 1613 he died there.

Throughout 1614 Carr rode on the crest of the wave. He was all in all to the King, leader of government in conjunction with the Howards. To his pride and self-confidence there were no bounds.

But Carr was too proud, too sure of his hold over James. When he saw a rival, George Villiers, coming up to challenge his place, he was scornful and too self-assured to notice the King's real interest in the newcomer. In the first months of 1615 James found it necessary to issue a warning to the Earl of Somerset that his arrogance might be his undoing:

For the easing of my inward and consuming grief, all I crave is, that in all the words and actions of your life you make it appear that you never think to hold me but out of love, and not one hair by force. Consider that I am a free man if I were not a king. Remember that all your being, except your breathing and soul, is from me. I told you twice or thrice you might lead me by the heart and not by the nose. If ever I find you think to retain me by one sparkle of fear, all the violence of my love will in that instant be changed into as violent a hatred.

God is my judge, my love hath been infinite towards you; and only the strength of my affection towards you hath made me bear these things and bridle my passion. Let me be met, then, with your entire heart but softened by humility. Let me never apprehend that you disdain my person and undervalue my qualities; and let it not appear that your former affection is cold towards me. Hold me thus by the heart; and you may build upon my favour as upon a rock.[2]

But still Somerset would not be chastened. When Villiers came to him, offering him service and friendship, the Earl disdained them. He began to spend long periods away from Court, with his alluring wife, yet unreasonably still expected James's entire devotion when he returned.

Then, in September 1615, a terrible scandal broke. Evidence had been brought to light that Overbury's death in the Tower had not been of natural causes: he had been poisoned. All the information which the royal government gathered pointed to the complicity of the Earl and Countess of Somerset.

The King, still loving Somerset (though Villiers was rising steadily), wept at the news, but conscience would not allow him to conceal his friend's crime. The Earl and Countess were sent into the Tower, to emerge only for their trial, in May 1616. Both were found guilty of Overbury's murder, as accessories before the fact; both were sentenced to death. All that day, during the trial, the King was on tenterhooks, cursing every boat which approached his palace at Greenwich which brought no tidings of his friends' fate; but when the news of the sentences came, James was very quiet.

In the days that followed, the King commuted the death-sentence to one of imprisonment in the Tower at his pleasure. In fact, the Somersets emerged in 1622, to go into country retirement together, but Robert Carr, Earl of Somerset did not return to Court, nor did James ever seek to see him again.

George Villiers, who had by then long since taken over Carr's role and who was to surpass him in influence, was a model of male beauty: tall and straight, he had lustrous chestnut hair and bright eyes; so fresh and brilliant was his complexion that the King fancied that he resembled St Stephen, described in the Bible as having a face which glowed "as it were the face of an angel": he called Villiers 'Steenie' thereafter.

Villiers had first caught James's roving eye in the summer of 1614, when he stood among the crowd of gentry at Apethorpe where the King was staying during his progress through the shires; but he might have remained in obscurity had it not been for the designs of the Protestant party who sought a rival for Carr.

The Herbert brothers (one of them that Philip who had once enjoyed the King's love himself) and the Archbishop of Canterbury were members of the cabal which planned to advance George Villiers: they even drew Queen Anne into their scheme, for she was no friend to Carr, who had often insulted her. Together they brought Villiers to the Court and, even before Carr disappeared from view, had won a knighthood for their protégé, seeing him advance steadily in royal service. The Howards tried to counter this attempt with candidates of their own choosing: Lady Suffolk was commissioned to seek out likely young men, whom she was reputed to be "tricking and pranking up", washing their faces with "curd posset" to make them shine like Villiers'. But her efforts went for nothing. James had no eyes for anyone but his Steenie.

Villiers was King James's last love, intelligent enough to find means of keeping the King's affection for a decade and to make himself indispensable in government. He quickly discarded his backers, making himself independent of their support and of royal backing by building up a party of his own, mainly comprising men dependent solely on him for their political, administrative and Court appointments.

The son of a mere country knight, his own education had been meagre, but he had sufficient native wit, according to a contemporary, "first to sift and question well and to supply his own defects by the drawing or flowing into him of the best instruments of experience and knowledge, from whom he had a sweet and attractive manner to suck what might be for the public or his own purpose".[3] Those two purposes were often indistinguishable: Villiers had a way of putting his finger on points of policy by the pursuit of which he might aggrandise himself while at the same time seeming to work for the public good. And he was ruthless in self-protection: when his own brothers were attacked in Parliament for their involvement in the iniquitous system of monopolies (by which men enriched themselves at the public expense), he dropped them without compunction. However, in the main, George Villiers was a tireless schemer for his family's enrichment: the King was open-handed with his favours to the Villiers connection, awarding titles and estates and heiress-brides with the utmost generosity. By the end of the reign, George Villiers had risen from knight to viscount, to earl, to marquess, to duke, while earldoms and viscounties were lavished on his mother and brothers.

Not once did James have cause to doubt Villiers' fidelity to him, not even after the young man's marriage to Catherine Manners, a placid, not overly-intelligent girl who adored her husband and who made a pleasing addition to the royal ménage as yet another 'daughter' to the King.

My only sweet and dear child [James wrote to Villiers, now Marquess of Buckingham, soon after his wedding],

Thy dear dad sends thee his blessing this morning and also to his daughter. The Lord of Heaven send you a sweet and blithe awakening, all kind of comfort in your sanctified bed and bless the fruits thereof, that I may have sweet bedchamber boys to play with me (and this is my daily prayer).

Sweet hearty, when thou riseth, keep thee from importunity of people that may trouble thy mind, that at meeting I may see thy white teeth shine upon me, and so bear me company in my journey; and so God bless thee.

James R.[4]

These were stormy years in politics and, were it not for the King's willingness to dispense with the services of his Parliaments, when they became too demanding of power, Villiers might have been overthrown by his enemies. As it was, he was safe in James's trust and increasingly came to determine the course of royal policy. His main aim, as the 1620s opened, was to effect a Spanish marriage for James's heir, his only surviving son Charles, as the culmination of his pretensions in diplomacy.

Prince Charles had once been the most bitter of Villiers' detractors, but, a teen-aged boy, with no power of his own, he could only play spiteful tricks to annoy his father's favourite (once he turned a fountain against Villiers, ruining the smart suit in which he peacocked). Then, suddenly, Charles fell under Villiers' spell. To the King's delight, the two young men became constant companions. James's generous nature allowed of no jealousy: he was only too glad to see 'Baby Charles' as devoted as he was himself to their Steenie.

Together, in 1623, the Prince and the royal favourite embarked for Spain on an exciting and romantic expedition to woo an infanta as Charles's bride, but for months they stayed on at Madrid, becoming ever more frustrated and irritable as the Spaniards haggled for the terms of their alliance, while King James sat in lonely solitude at home, fearful that Spain would make his boys prisoners or turn them into Catholics. When they returned, his joy was boundless, even though they arrived without the royal bride and breathing fire and fury against the perfidy of Spain, which boded ill for the King's policy of alliance.

Now James was old. He allowed Buckingham and Charles to dictate his policies. They brought England to the very brink of war with Spain.

George Villiers, now Duke of Buckingham, had many enemies, who did not hesitate to carry tales against him to the King. But James would believe nothing against his Steenie. Towards the end of his life, in December 1624, the King wrote to the young Duke:

I pray God that I may have a joyful and comfortable meeting with you, and that we may make this Christenmass a new marriage, ever to be kept hereafter; for, God so love me, as I desire only to live in this world for your sake, and that I had rather live banished in any part of the world with you than live a sorrowful widow-life without you. And so God bless you, my sweet child and wife, and grant that ye may ever be a comfort to your old dad and husband.[5]

Buckingham's feelings for the King are less certain. They were evinced, seemingly sincerely, in the affectionate, teasing letters which he addressed to James, but then the Duke must always please his benefactor. Inevitably, the elderly lover would be regarded more for his ability to enrich and aggrandise than for his personal merits to affection. And there was, apparently, little in the King's person to stimulate sexual desire.

He was of middle stature [wrote a contemporary], more corpulent though in his clothes than in his body, yet fat enough, his clothes being ever made large and easy, the doublets quilted for stiletto-proof, his breeches in great pleats and full stuffed. He was naturally of timorous disposition, which was the reason of his quilted doublets; his eyes were rolling after any stranger come into his presence. His beard was very thin. His tongue too large for his mouth, which ever made him speak full in the mouth and made him drink very uncomely, as if eating his drink, which came out into the cup at each side of his mouth.
His skin was soft as taffeta sarsnet, which felt so because he never washed his hands, only rubbed his fingers and slightly with the wet end of a napkin.[6]

Tottering on his spindly legs, his head lolling and his eyes rolling, exuding an odour of rank sweat, King James VI of Scotland and I of England was not a pleasant sight. His humour was broad, pawky and bawdy; his learning was deep but pedantic; he could be noisy and raucous, but also sentimental and maudlin; he was often ill, often irritable. And yet for years Buckingham accepted the King's caresses along with his gifts, never failing to accord James that devotion which he craved. Whatever the physical relations between George Villiers and the King, the younger man seemed to find his exertions worthwhile in terms of financial reward and access to power.

Buckingham's ascendancy over Prince Charles ensured that his influence would continue into the next reign, but it is extremely unlikely that their friendship was ever based on sexual relations: the Prince was high-principled and fastidious, proving later that he was both heterosexual and monogamous; he was to have enemies who would condemn every facet of his rule, but they could find no stone to cast at his sexual morals. The Prince's relationship with Buckingham was apparently that of a Jonathan to the more vibrant personality's David; intense and emotional as that relationship was, it did not involve physical relations.

By 1625, Villiers was secure in Charles's affections and could look to a future under the new King in which his own honours and influence could only increase: the tedious, querulous old man to whom he owed everything was now dispensable.

Buckingham's enemies claimed that he murdered King James by poisoning him. It is impossible now to prove or disprove the charge, but the crime seems feasible and in character. It is certainly possible that Buckingham could have poisoned the King, though more likely that he took advantage of a natural illness, weakening the already sick man with the potions prepared for him by the doctors whom he called in: the Duke and his mother undertook all the nursing themselves, supported by physicians of their own choosing—an inviting opportunity for foul play.

King James went into a high fever from which he did not recover. He died on 27 March 1625.

Just over three years of life then remained to George Villiers, Duke of Buckingham. Under King Charles I, he acquired ever more power, but now, with Parliament becoming increasingly vociferous against the monarchy's vaunted prerogatives and against the favourite's influence, he had to face up to his enemies at last. There was even an attempt by the Commons to impeach him, which failed only because the King, fearful for his friend's life, dissolved Parliament. Buckingham tried to redeem his reputation and win popularity by leading a military expedition to France, to aid Protestant Frenchmen (the Huguenots) against their Catholic king. Victory would have made him a hero in England, but in action at La Rochelle and the Ile de Rhé, Buckingham suffered ignominious defeat. His waste of treasury money and Englishmen's lives caused an outcry at home: his personal bravery in battle was ignored.

Then, in the summer of 1628, a naval officer named John Felton bought himself a dagger and set out to walk from London to Portsmouth to find Buckingham, bitter against the man who had sent so many of his friends to their death in France, and who had, he believed, denied him the promotion which was his due. In his hat was concealed a letter in which he made his apologia for the crime he intended to commit:

That man is cowardly and base and deserveth not the name of a gentleman or soldier that is not willing to sacrifice his life for the honour of his God, his king and his country. Let no man commend me for doing of it, but rather discommend themselves as the cause of it, for if God had not taken away our hearts for our sins, he would not have gone so long unpunished.[7]

As the Duke of Buckingham walked out of his dining-room after breakfast on the morning of 18 August, Felton stepped out from behind a curtain and, crying "God have mercy upon thy soul!", plunged his dagger into Buckingham's left side. The Duke staggered a few paces, trying to pull the knife out, but blood came pouring from his mouth and he collapsed. A few moments later, he died.

King Charles was staying in a house a few miles away, at Southwick, and he was at prayers when the messenger from Portsmouth arrived. Someone approached him, whispered the news and retired. The King did not move. When the service ended, he walked into his own room and closed the door. Only then did he break down: all through that day, his courtiers could hear him sobbing.

In the days that followed, while Charles came to terms with his grief and with the prospect of future life without Steenie, the nation roared out its joy and thanked God for the brave assassin.

One person who had good cause to greet the news of Buckingham's death with smiles was the young Queen, Henrietta Maria, a French princess whom Charles had married soon after his accession. She had come to hate her husband's favourite, and to fear that Charles's absorption in Buckingham would always preclude her from his love. While the Duke lived, he took care to foment quarrels between the King and Queen, lest Henrietta Maria should set up as a rival for Charles's affections, and he packed her household with his own kindred, spying on her every movement.

But Buckingham died soon enough for the royal marriage to be saved: it is significant that, though Henrietta Maria had failed to conceive before, within weeks of his death she was found to be pregnant. The King and Queen became a model of marital love.

The Duke died soon enough also for Charles to have saved his throne as well as his marriage. Without the unpopular counsellor at his elbow, he might now have turned to wiser men who could have shown him the error of his anachronistic views on the role of monarchy.

These views were largely the product of James I's strictures to his son on the powers and rights of kings, their 'divine right' as it was known, which made them accountable to no one but God. Charles applied these doctrines firmly in his government, paying no heed to the growing independence and power-hunger of his Parliaments. Complex theories, complex motives, brought England, in the 1640s, into two armed camps, with the King and the Parliament as declared enemies. The great Civil War ensued, and in 1649 Charles I died under the headsman's axe, victim of his own political crimes.

Many of Buckingham's detractors have sought to show that his ambition and its fulfilment were the prime causes of the hostility between King and Parliament: they have overstated their case. The Duke's avarice, his obsession with self-fulfilment through power, and his hold over the two kings, were enough to alienate the vast mass of politically-conscious Englishmen, and in 1628 loyalty to the monarchy was at a low ebb; but, after Buckingham's death, Charles had innumerable chances to come to terms with his subjects: that he would not was his own responsibility, the outcome of his own character and principles.

Nevertheless, though Buckingham's place in English history may be less important than was once supposed, it was considerable in comparison with that of his predecessors among James Stuart's favourites, and his name will never be omitted from any study of the nation's political and constitutional development.

7

Old Rowley

" 'Cuckolds all awry!' The old dance of England!" cried King Charles II,[1] commanding his musicians to strike up a country dance whose name could as well have been applied to his own Court. And just as Charles had the first choice of partners in the ballroom, so he had in his bedroom.

In the reign of King Charles II the English Court became a by-word for sexual promiscuity, and, while almost every nobleman had his mistress and his bastards, none could rival the King's sexual prowess and virility. He never tired of the chase, never lost his taste for novelty: he was a natural polygamist. There were even jokes and lewd verses hailing him as 'Old Rowley', a nickname earned by his supposedly equalling the feats and stamina of a goat of that name, tethered on the palace green.

Charles was the 'merry monarch' of 'merry England': he had an exuberance, a vitality, which buoyed him up even in the most trying circumstances; a casual charm combined with a credible sincerity, impressive even to such men of integrity as the visionary Quaker William Penn; but above all, and unlike any other Stuart monarch of the era, he had none of the Stuarts' self-consciousness and self-deception, but could look at himself and laugh at himself. As a monarch, Charles II was less than perfect; as a moral being, there was much in his life which measured up to neither contemporary nor modern standards: but it is impossible wholly to dislike or despise what he was, and eminently possible to be admiring of his many virtues.

He was not always the soft-living, self-indulgent man whom we see in 1660–85, the years of his reign: his childhood had passed in the formal and tranquil Court of his father, Charles I, but at the age of twelve the future Charles II was thrown into the hurly-burly of politics and war, into a life of alternating labour and idleness in which not only his next meal but his very survival was frequently uncertain.

He was just over two months past his twelfth birthday when, in August 1642, his father signified the opening of the great Civil War by raising his standard over Nottingham Castle. For three years afterwards he rode through England in the army's wake, as the Royalists engaged the rebel Parliamentarians in battle after battle. He was fifteen when his father's failing fortunes caused the King to send him to safety abroad. From 1646 until 1660 (apart from a brief, disastrous excursion into Scotland and England in 1650–51), Charles lived in exile on the Continent.

The Prince of these years was not yet the elegant, debonair man of later fame. In his late teens he was tall and gangling, sallow and heavy-browed, taciturn and ill-at-ease in the brilliant French Court at which he joined his exiled mother. His buxom, capricious, strong-willed cousin Anne Marie Louise de Montpensier found Charles *gauche* and *jejeune*, affecting not to speak or understand French; in his turn, the Prince did not take to 'la Grande Mademoiselle'; he liked his women lively, as she was, but not so overbearing. Soon, he was to be found in the less taxing company of the delightful Isabelle Angelique, Duchesse de Châtillon, his 'Bablon', as he called her, who was to sweeten his time in France without making any demands on him.

According to one story, which seems to have been apocryphal, Charles had gained his first sexual experience at the age of sixteen, during his stay on the island of Jersey in the summer of 1646, when he was *en route* to France. His first mistress, we are told, was Margaret de Carteret, daughter of one of the island's *seigneurs*, and, we are asked to believe, she bore him a son, named James de la Cloche, who many years later became a Catholic priest, a member of the Society of Jesus. But the existence of this first of Charles's many bastards, and indeed the story of the *affaire* itself, rests on some letters between father and son found in the Jesuits' archives in the nineteenth century—they are almost certainly spurious.

It is also alleged that the young Duke of Buckingham (son of James I's and Charles I's favourite) debauched the future Charles II in Paris soon after his arrival, introducing him to the pleasures of the town. Buckingham was certainly a prematurely experienced young man, who had known the sex-sodden Courts of the Italian princes, but we need not accord to him the blame of the future King's vices, for he was only briefly in Paris during Charles's first stay there, and Queen Henrietta Maria was keeping her son under strict control, with an eye to Mademoiselle's dowry.

Nevertheless, it soon became obvious that Charles would not emulate his father's purity. In the last months of Charles I's life, while the King was awaiting trial by Parliament, the Prince was courting a young Welsh girl, Lucy Walter. In April 1649, three months after the King was executed and her lover succeeded to his empty title, Lucy gave birth to a son; within a year two more royal bastards had been borne by Catherine Pegge and Elizabeth Killigrew, ladies of the Court in exile which was daily increasing in size as defeated Cavaliers fled from the new regime in England. By the year 1657, it was said that Lady Byron was the young King's seventeenth mistress abroad.

One might safely speculate that Charles took his first mistresses not only for his lust but also to find in warm, dark embraces an escape from the bitter misery of his situation. He had to wait, powerless, while his father was held prisoner in England; to be ready, on any day, to hear of the King's death on the block; then to accept the transference of loyalty of hundreds of Royalists, penniless and hungry, who milled around him in hopes of some reward for their past service in the war; to balance the already fierce rivalries of his counsellors; and, above all, to take on the ultimate responsibility for continuing a seemingly hopeless campaign against the Parliamentarian regime at home, which every day became more firmly entrenched. It is surely no wonder, therefore, that he snatched what hours of respite he could from such overwhelming problems, finding distraction, even oblivion, in the arms of such as Lucy Walter and her successors.

The contemporary diarist Evelyn gave his opinion that Lucy, whose surname he thought was Barlow, was "a brown, beautiful, bold but insipid creature", "a beautiful strumpet", "the daughter of some very mean creatures"[2]: in fact, Barlow was an alias which she sometimes used, and she was not meanly born but the daughter of a gentleman of considerable property in Wales. There is no doubt of her beauty: her few portraits show her

with attractive features, bright eyes and shining brown hair;
and she was certainly a "strumpet": she had arrived in Holland,
where she met Charles, as the mistress of one man, Colonel
Sydney, who, it was said, soon afterwards sold her to his
brother before she was taken up by the Prince; however, there
must be doubt as to whether Lucy Walter was ever "insipid":
her relations with her royal lover do not suggest that at all.

How long Charles and Lucy lived together after the birth of
their son seems uncertain. It is evident that they were apart for
long stretches between 1649 and 1651, when the new King was
travelling, in hopes first of all of mounting an invasion of his
kingdoms and then vainly attempting this venture, but whether
they settled down together on his return is open to doubt.
During the King's brief stay in Scotland in 1650–51, the dour
Presbyterians had attempted his moral reform, and it was
obvious that his reputation as a lecher was a stumbling-block
to their whole-hearted loyalty, so that on his return to the
Continent, even his more broad-minded English counsellors
advocated discretion, and from this time began a campaign to
part him from Lucy. Certainly they had little trouble in blacken-
ing her character in their reports to the King: even in his
absence she had taken lovers, and had given birth to a daughter
whom Charles would never accept as his own. Still, he may have
resorted to her occasionally, according to her own evidence later.

In 1656, 'Mrs Barlow' suddenly appeared in England, accompanied by her then lover Colonel Howard, spending so freely
and putting on such style that she was soon suspected as a
Royalist spy. She tried to convince the authorities that she
had not seen Charles in two years, that her son by him was
dead, but, when her own maid informed against her, she was
sent to the Tower.

Lord Protector Cromwell may have realised that Lucy free
would be more trouble to the King than Lucy a prisoner. He
had her released and deported, but made very useful propaganda
out of the plight of Charles's 'lady of pleasure', as she was
termed, only confirming the prejudices of Puritan and puri-
tanical Commonwealthmen.

For some time after her return to the Continent, Lucy and
her son James were placed in the care of royal servants, who,
under the King's instructions, ransacked her boxes for papers
which, she claimed, proved their marriage and the legitimacy

of their son. Apparently they either failed to discover such documents or secretly destroyed them, for Charles felt safe enough to discard his mistress completely, and after some unpleasant public hysterics from Lucy, to have young 'Jacky' taken away from her and sent off to Paris. His mother followed him, only to die soon after, penniless and miserable, according to moralising contemporaries.

King Charles preferred women who had the sophistication to enjoy their royal favours without demanding too much of his emotions—such as 'Bablon' de Châtillon, whose relations with him continued over several years without demands of fidelity by either party. Wherever the King went—and he wandered back and forth between the Spanish Netherlands and the United Provinces, down the Rhine and, later, into Spain, during his exile—there were pretty women glad to comply with the royal request for their bodies.

During the 1650s, the Royalists in England and Scotland made several attempts to overthrow the Cromwellian regime, always unsuccessfully. It was only after Oliver Cromwell's death, and after the failure of his son Richard to keep control of the government after the breach between Parliament and Army that conditions in England and Scotland were favourable to a restoration of the monarchy. Men feared anarchy in the unstable conditions which obtained in 1659 and were only too ready to accede to the demands of the powerful General Monck that King Charles should be called home.

He landed at Dover on 25 May 1660, and, the story goes, he spent his first night in his kingdom in the arms of the beautiful Barbara Villiers.

Barbara Villiers was the granddaughter of a half-brother of the first Duke of Buckingham. A typical product of her family, she had good looks, charm, intelligence—and overweening self-love. Some twenty years old at the Restoration, she had recently been the mistress of the Earl of Chesterfield and for about a year the wife of a minor Royalist agent in England, Roger Palmer. She had gone to Charles's Court at Brussels as a courier for Palmer's masters, the conspirators known as the Sealed Knot, and it had not taken her long to catch the King's eye. When Charles returned to England to receive his crown, Barbara went with him, to enjoy the rewards of her position.

The King was totally enthralled by his mistress, but policy

dictated that he must have a wife, to ensure, by her giving him sons, the succession to the throne. However, no one thought that the wife would exclude the mistress, and when the royal bride, Princess Catherine of Portugal, arrived in England, it was to find Barbara Villiers firmly ensconced in Charles's affections and in leadership of his Court, the mother of one royal bastard and pregnant with another. Catherine had been warned that this would be the case, and she was determined from the outset to oust Barbara, now Countess of Castlemaine.

The King had named his mistress as one of his wife's ladies-in-waiting, but Queen Catherine would have none of it. There were quarrels and scenes, but neither husband nor wife would give way. When Charles led Barbara in to be presented to Catherine, the unhappy wife did not realise at first who she was and graciously extended her hand: then, perhaps alerted by the sniggers of courtiers, she understood, falling back in a faint, her nose bleeding profusely.

For weeks the King and Queen were at loggerheads over 'the Lady', and it seemed that there would be an irremediable breach between them. But, for all her love for Charles and her piety, Catherine was realistic. An observer wrote: "The Queen on a sudden let herself fall first into conversation and then to familiarity, and even in the same instant to a confidence with the Lady; was merry with her in public, talked kindly to her, and in private used nobody more friendly."[3] The King was delighted: he became kinder to his wife, realising and respecting her affection. Catherine never gave him children (to the Queen's chagrin, Barbara proved embarrassingly fecund, with three sons and two daughters acknowledged by their royal father), but despite statesmen's pleas that he should divorce her and marry a woman who could give him an heir, Charles would never repudiate Catherine. He always insisted on her dignities as Queen, devastating Barbara Villiers with his anger when she dared to insult his wife, and giving Catherine what affection he had to spare from his more passionate *amours*.

Though Barbara Villiers never managed wholly to fill Charles's vision, his interest in her rarely flagged for long. Even when she was in advanced pregnancy, certainly not looking her best, Barbara's charm received the tribute of her lover's visits at suppertime most evenings, and she never had cause to complain that he was ungenerous: while she amassed the most enviable fortune in property and jewels, her children were ennobled into the forefront of the English peerage.

However, Lady Castlemaine was a tiring companion. The King was easy-going, hard to rouse to anger, but Barbara was temperamental and volatile, frequently heard to scream like a fishwife when crossed. And she was a confirmed meddler, fond of imagining her influence over Charles to be greater than it was: certainly she was instrumental in obtaining the advancement of her friend Sir Henry Bennet to the position of Secretary of State, and certainly she was courted by hopeful politicians and foreign diplomats alike, for her unique opportunities of assisting them in royal favour, but she had no permanent, formal party, and no consistent policy can be ascribed to her protégés. This Villiers could never rival the first Duke of Buckingham in power over the monarchy.

The reign of Barbara Villiers lasted some eight years, but that is not to say that she had no rivals. King Charles found no cause, from conscience or reason, to control his desires and their fulfilment, and though there remained a Puritan element always within his realms, it had no concerted voice to rebuke him with any force. The pursuit of love became to Charles II an absorbing game, in which his emotions, though often engaged, took second place to physical urges. He took his pleasure where it was offered, or where he could persuade it, and not one of his discarded mistresses seems to have held rancour against him for long.

In the main, his mistresses were women of the world, knowing the rules of the game and the prizes. Most of them were Court ladies, wives of courtiers or maids-of-honour from the Queen's household (such as the complaisant Win Wells, who reputedly suffered a miscarriage of a royal child in the midst of a Court ball but recovered sufficiently to dance on, unconcerned, leaving the foetus on the floor).

In fact, the promiscuous career of the King of England was remarkably similar to that of his French cousin Louis XIV. Both had the pick of the beauties of their Courts, and neither was ever without a mistress. While Charles was under the sway of Barbara Villiers, Louis had his Louise de la Vallière, the first of his *maîtresses-en-titre*, who was replaced in about 1671 by Athenaïs de Montespan, neither of whom excluded interesting interludes with Mesdames and Mesdemoiselles de Soubise, de Ludres, de Fontanges, Doré, Oeillets and Thianges and several more. Unlike Charles, however, Louis reformed in middle age, under the influence of his second wife, the pious and serious Françoise de Maintenon, whom he married in 1683.

The two kings were always close in sympathy, even when their ministers were hot for an Anglo-French war, and for years Charles accepted a pension from his cousin as pledge for his future conversion to the Catholic Church: in fact, the King may well have been serious about this, but he was sufficiently realistic to know that his kingdoms would never permit any more tolerance against Catholics than the little which existed. However, his secret pact with Louis held good.

The cousins' friendship was cemented by their mutual love for Charles's youngest sister, Henrietta Anne, who had been married in her mid-teens to the French king's younger brother, Philippe, Duke of Orleans. Philippe was homosexual and transvestite, but fiercely possessive of his petite and charming wife, and when Louis fell in love with his sister-in-law, his dangerous attentions to her were only diverted by her offering him her maid-of-honour Louise de la Vallière in her place: but she had tact, the little Duchess, and never lost the French King's regard, which she employed to good use in her mediations between him and her brother. Between Charles and 'Minette' (his own pet-name for her) there was a strong bond: the King was a devoted family man, but he loved his young sister with an unusual intensity, writing to her frequently with a facile pen from which endearments and secrets flowed.

It was to the Duchess that the King owed his introduction to the beautiful Frances Stuart, a distant cousin of the royal family who had been in Minette's household in France and whom she sent over to serve her sister-in-law in 1663. But here, for once, Charles found a woman not aware of the honour bestowed on her by his lust: time and again she rebuffed his advances.

Frances was only fifteen years old when she arrived in England, but already she was an outstanding beauty. Until recently the coinage of Britain bore witness to her classic profile: the King had the engraver Roettier immortalise her as Britannia, in which guise she appeared for years on copper coins.

While Charles's boon companions formed "a committee for the getting of Mistress Stuart for the King", even Lady Castle-

maine was forced to further her lover's desires: more than once
he let it be known that he would not sup with his mistress
unless her rival sat at table with them. In fact, Barbara recognised the fact that Frances Stuart, mistress or no mistress, was
no real rival to her own power, for she was a mere adolescent,
for all her French-acquired veneer of sophistication, and not
well endowed with intelligence. Perhaps to prevent more clever
women from possessing the King, perhaps to cover her own
amours, Lady Castlemaine titillated Charles's fancy even further
by making Frances her constant companion: often the King
would come upon them lying together in bed of a morning.

With amazing will-power, Frances Stuart held out against
Charles's protestations of love. Then, suddenly, in March 1668,
she eloped with another Charles Stuart (another royal cousin),
Duke of Richmond and Lennox, who had offered her marriage.
The King was hurt and angry: "You may think me ill-natured,"
he wrote to his sister in France, "but if you consider how hard
a thing 'tis to swallow an injury done by a person I had so much
tenderness for, you will in some degree excuse the resentment
I used towards her."[5] From the manuscript letter, it is obvious
that the King had originally written the word 'love' and thought
better of it, substituting that word 'tenderness'. For months he
refused to receive the couple; only when he heard that the
Duchess was ill with smallpox, likely to die, did he relent, and
later rejoiced in her recovery, admitting the Richmonds to
favour.

It was widely suspected that Lady Castlemaine had connived
at the elopement, to rid herself of a rival whose tantalising
attractions she felt she could not combat much longer. And
she made double capital from it by joining the party against
another of its promoters, Lord Chancellor Clarendon, against
whom she had long nursed bitter grudges: Clarendon was the
father-in-law of James, Duke of York, Charles's brother and
heir, and it was thought that he feared the Duke's displace-
ment in the royal succession should the King, as was rumoured,
divorce Queen Catherine and marry Frances, who would give
Charles a son to take James's place. There were many other,
more definite factors in Clarendon's fall of 1668, but Lady
Castlemaine's spite and her leadership of the party against him
was certainly a considerable part of it.

However, she did not long survive her old enemy. Scarcely had

Clarendon fled the country than Barbara found herself paid off with an excellent estate close to the Palace—which would mean that she no longer needed her apartments there, from which she had been wont to keep a tyrannical eye on the King's movements. Two years later she was created Duchess of Cleveland, with great estates and pensions. But apart from Charles's care for their children's careers, that was the end of his involvement with Barbara. She had been taking other lovers for years, from courtiers down to one Jacob Hall, a tight-rope walker, and now she was freer to go her own way, though until the end of the reign she would return to Court on occasion and seemed on good terms with the King. She lived on until 1709, ironically impoverished not by her own extravagance but by the depredations of her fortune wrought by 'Beau' Feilding, a scoundrel ten years her junior who married her bigamously when she was sixty-four years old.

It was at about the time of Barbara's fall from favour, or just before it, that the King widened his circle to embrace two actresses, Moll Davis and Nell Gwyn. Moll, a musical comedy actress, was reputedly a bastard of the great Howard family, but 'sweet Nell of old Drury' had no such pretensions: she was a Cockney born and bred, once a barmaid in a brothel who had graduated from selling oranges in London theatres to treading their boards in comic parts. Her wit became famous, to the discomfort of her many butts.

One of them was the next of the King's chief mistresses, Louise de Keroualle. She was a beauty, no one could deny it, but she had a slight cast in one eye, which gave Nell the chance to dub her 'Squintabella'. Also, Louise was a snob: the daughter of a minor nobleman of Brittany, she claimed kinship with far greater aristocrats and went into mourning at the death of a supposed cousin—Nell immediately donned black for 'the Grand Cham of Tartary'. But Louise could afford to ignore Nell Gwyn's mockery: Charles loaded her with jewels and estates and, in 1673, created her Duchess of Portsmouth. Barbara Villiers' three sons became dukes, as did Nell's elder son, but Louise's boy, Charles, was created Duke of Richmond, with precedence over his half-brothers.

The King had first seen Louise in the train of his sister Minette, when the Duchess had come to England in 1670 to negotiate the secret Treaty of Dover between him and Louis

XIV. Minette had refused to leave the simple, unsullied Louise in her brother's tender care, despite his pleas, but the King's beloved sister died soon after her return to France, and, not long afterwards, King Louis sent the girl over to England, on the pretext of placing her in Queen Catherine's household, to make her Minette's successor as watchdog on the alliance. However, Louise's supposed influence on Charles II had little substance: in fact, she was a continual irritant to the anti-French party at Court. Also, during anti-Catholic disturbances, she was a reminder to politicians and populace of the King's suspected French Catholic sympathies. (When the mob attacked the supposed carriage of the Duchess of Portsmouth on one occasion, they were deterred by the sight of Nell Gwyn instead, shouting from the window that they should know better for she was 'the Protestant whore'.)

Louise remained as the royal *maîtresse-en-titre* until the end of Charles II's life, though she had to share his body with other women. One of them, who briefly eclipsed Louise, was the Italian beauty Hortense Mancini, Duchess of Mazarin, who had married a French noble of such ostentatious and masochistic piety that his rigorous disciplines drove her to flee his company and from France. She had already had a colourful career, roaming Europe, when she arrived in England in 1676, to add Charles's name to the long list of her lovers.

But Nell's going into mourning, this time for Louise's lost favour, was premature. Fierce as was the King's passion for Hortense at first, it soon burned out, and the Duchess of Portsmouth was once again supreme.

Queen Catherine had long since ceased to complain at the number of her husband's mistresses and the friendliness she was expected to show to them. In general she was discreet, rarely visiting the King's bedroom uninvited lest she surprise him with a companion: only once did she do so, laughing when she discovered a lady's slipper under the bed and withdrawing at once so that "the pretty fool", as she said, could come out of hiding.

But if the King's untiring consideration and affection to her could soothe Catherine's jealousy of his mistresses, nothing could compensate her for her lack of children. She suffered several miscarriages and, by the late 1660s, it was obvious that she would never give Charles an heir to his throne. It was often suggested to him that he divorce her, remarry and beget a legitimate heir, but he always refused to do so. The nation's history might have been very different indeed if Charles had been less soft-hearted. . . .

On the last day of January 1685, the diarist Evelyn took a look at the Court:

. . . I am never to forget the unexpressible luxury and profaneness, gaming and all dissolution and, as it were, total forgetfulness of God (it being Sunday evening) which . . . I was witness of: the King sitting and toying with his concubines Portsmouth, Cleveland and Mazarin, etc; a French boy singing love-songs in the glorious gallery, whilst about twenty of the great courtiers and other dissolute persons were at basset [a gambling game] round a large table, a bank of at least two thousand in gold before them, upon which two gentlemen that were with me made reflections with astonishment, it being a scene of utmost vanity, and surely, as they thought, would never have an end.[5]

But there was to be an end very soon. The next day the King was taken ill, and on 6 February he died. As Evelyn concluded, "all was in the dust".

King Monmouth

The year 1685 witnessed an event unique in the nation's history: a royal bastard challenging for the throne, when, at the death of Charles II, his eldest son, James, Duke of Monmouth, took up arms against his uncle, the legitimate heir, James II. Not that Monmouth would have allowed himself to be thought of as either bastard or pretender: he had become convinced that he was legitimate (he may even have had forged papers to prove it), that only his father's hopes of seeing the Catholic Church restored in his kingdoms by his brother James of York had prevented his acknowledging his Protestant son James of Monmouth as his heir.

Apart from their religion, there was little to choose between the two Jameses in their personal suitability to reign: the Duke of York was stolid, unimaginative, stubborn, totally unconcerned (as he would prove after initial assurances to the contrary) by his subjects' sensibilities in politics and religion; the Duke of Monmouth was dashing and romantic, gullible and biddable, brave but foolhardy. Even their own supporters in the days of their rivalry under Charles II, considered both men a liability to their respective parties.

The Duke of Monmouth had gathered a good deal of loyalty during the last decade of his father's reign. He had been taken up by the brilliant statesman the Earl of Shaftesbury, a power-greedy man who used England's fear of Catholicism to brew up a potent draught of violence, drunk by honest men as well as his own henchmen. In the late 1670s Shaftesbury was responsible not only for the turmoil in Parliament in favour of the exclusion of the Catholic Duke of York from the royal succession but also for whipping up hysterical outbursts of anti-Catholic feeling, which resulted in rioting, attacks on Catholic houses and businesses and a series of state trials of leading Catholic figures.

The Earl's adoption of Monmouth as his candidate for the

throne was accepted even by those who claimed to support 'legitimist' principles, for the thought of the alternative heir was abhorrent to the majority of Englishmen and Scotsmen of the time.

Monmouth himself was a popular figurehead for the movement. Having been taken from his mother, Lucy Walter, at an early age, he had been brought up largely under the eye of his paternal grandmother, Queen Henrietta Maria, until the Restoration brought him home to his father's Court. There, he had been treated with almost princely honours and loaded with Court and state offices. He had inherited much of his father's casual charm and many of his attractive vices; he was amusing, witty, athletic and an accomplished dancer, free with his money (or rather, with that of the wealthy Scottish heiress his wife), familiar with his friends and subordinates, and a notable womaniser. He had taken his pick of maids-of-honour in the 1670s (one, Eleanor Needham, gave him four children), and only in 1680 found a woman to whom he could be faithful: Henrietta, Baroness Wentworth, who was to stand by him through his subsequent misfortunes and who died a year after Monmouth himself, aged twenty-five, reputedly of her grief.

But more valuable than the popularity which the Duke of Monmouth won in Court circles, was the respect which he gained in the group in Parliament and government who had recently been styled 'Whigs', the Protestant element led by Shaftesbury. As commander-in-chief of the army, James had suppressed the Covenanters' rebellion in Scotland but had been so notably merciful to the defeated that he had even increased his standing with the Whigs, who had sympathy with religious dissidents in the northern kingdom. When the Duke toured the provinces, he was everywhere hailed as "the Protestant hope", even as Prince of Wales, by the mob whose loyalty he and Shaftesbury long courted for future use.

There can be no doubt but that Charles II was extremely fond of his son, but he was bitterly hurt by the Duke's alignment with the Whigs and by his betrayal of the royal succession, which he saw as disloyalty to himself. When, in 1679, the King fell dangerously ill, so obvious was the intention of Monmouth and his friends of seizing the throne should Charles die, that when he did, in fact, recover, he was persuaded to deprive his son of his post as commander-in-chief (by which he might have raised the army against his uncle the Duke of York) and to order him to leave England. With characteristic foolhardiness, Monmouth returned home—uninvited by his father—before the end of the year, posturing and swaggering while the mob rang London bells and lit bonfires to hail his arrival.

But even worse was Monmouth's complicity in the Rye House Plot of March 1683—its aim to assassinate Charles and the Duke of York and to put the royal bastard on the throne. The failure of this enterprise ended the career of Shaftesbury, who fled abroad and died soon after, and it might have brought Monmouth himself to the block. Warrants were issued for his arrest on charges of high treason, but he evaded capture and went into hiding, soon afterwards bombarding the King with letters, in which he acknowledged some guilt but denied ever seeking the death of his father and uncle.

> I do call God Almighty to witness, and I wish I may die this moment I am writing, if ever it entered into my head, or I ever said the least thing to anybody that could make them think I could wish such a thing. . . .
> What good can it do you, Sir, to take your own child's life away, that only erred and ventured his life to save yours? And now, Sir, I do swear to you that from this time I never will displeasure you in anything; but the whole study of my life shall be to show you how truly penitent I am for having done it.[1]

Thus, while other men were brought to account for their part in the plot, Monmouth went free, fully pardoned.

Even then, however, the young Duke did not realise his good fortune but continued in his agitations against the Duke of York's supporters. By the turn of the same year, he was forced to leave the country, but the fond father sent him secret kind messages, even money for his support in the Netherlands.

Despite his professions of 1683 of loyalty to his uncle, when Monmouth heard of his father's death in February 1685 and of York's accession as James II, he began to lay his plans for an invasion of England and Scotland. It was to be a two-pronged attack, with his new friends the Scottish Covenanters to sweep south into England, the Duke himself to lead a force up from the west country to London. Thus, four months after the death of Charles II, on the evening of 11 June, he landed at Lyme in Dorset and raised his standard.

The Monmouth Rebellion lasted less than a month. In the

north, the royal army, forewarned, captured its leader, the Duke of Argyll, and rounded up its captains for transportation to the colonies. In the south, there was initially more success, with even royal militiamen flocking to Monmouth, but still their army was outnumbered when at last it met up with James's at Sedgemoor in Somerset.

Monmouth decided for a surprise attack on the royal encampment under cover of darkness, and this typically daring move might have been successful had he been in command of the royal army itself and not a band of inexperienced yokels under officers infinitely inferior to himself in on-the-ground soldiering. In the dark, his forces came up to a seemingly insuperable river, the Bussex Rhine: in fact it was only one of the wide ditches which cross the moor. They halted there, only yards away from the royal army, and when dawn came, the motley army, with its pitch-forks and scythes, was mown down by the superior force's artillery and cavalry. Monmouth fled, leaving his supporters to their fate.

A few days later he was found, shivering and hungry, in the New Forest.

Monmouth could expect no mercy from his uncle. For years James had regarded the Duke as his enemy, even his would-be assassin after the Rye House Plot's discovery. And the recent rebellion in two kingdoms had been compounded by Monmouth's proclamation of the King's guilt for all the nation's recent misfortunes, even the Great Fire of London of 1666. Monmouth grovelled at the King's feet, but he was treated with scorn. On 15 July 1685 he was beheaded. The famous executioner Jack Ketch was employed for the job, but in the face of a crowd of spectators notably sympathetic to Monmouth, the man bungled: it took him five blows of the axe to kill him, and even then the head had not been wholly severed: he finished his work with his knife.

Meanwhile, in the west country, the rebels had been dealt with in the most brutal manner. Many of the survivors of the battle were executed on the spot, others were held in custody until the arrival of 'Bloody Judge Jeffreys', the Lord Chief Justice and formerly King James's personal solicitor, who sentenced some three hundred of Monmouth's supporters to being hanged, drawn and quartered; hundreds more were transported to the West Indies.

And so, in blood and tears, ended the pretensions of the royal bastard.

The Monmouth Rebellion and its aftermath ensured, for the immediate future, a cowed people and a Parliament willing to prove its loyalty to James II by submission to royal policies. And by all the King's professions, it seemed that he was eager to be a good and popular monarch. At first even his Catholicism seemed to many a good omen, for it meant that he was sympathetic to others who had suffered for their religious dissent—and there remained many Puritans who had never accommodated themselves to the Anglican Church of the post-Restoration years. However, it soon became apparent that the King was bent on dragging his realms back into obedience to Rome, overturning the established Church and the Constitution. He tried to buy conversions by the offer of high office to noblemen and politicians; he attempted to pack Parliament with his supporters; he kept a standing army which, it was feared, he would turn on anyone defying his new policies; he appointed to bishoprics and key ecclesiastical posts men who, if not actually Catholics, were tending that way, and struck at churchmen who opposed him. The key to James II's failure was not his political ineptitude (though that was bad enough) but his total commitment to his personal faith and his obsession with its forcible extension throughout his kingdoms.

And this personal faith and commitment he owed not only to influences from his pre-Restoration years in Catholic countries on the Continent but in large measure to the influence of one woman: his mistress and later wife, Anne Hyde.

Anne was the daughter of that Edward Hyde who had served Charles II so tirelessly and zealously as Secretary of State during his years of exile, and through her family's close connexion with the royal family had been accorded a post as maid-of-honour to the King's sister Mary, Princess of Orange, in the 1650s. It was in the royal service that she first met James, Duke of York, and, in about 1657 or 1658, became his mistress. However, so discreet were the couple that nothing was known of the *affaire* until the summer after Charles II's restoration when it became obvious that Anne was pregnant.

Edward Hyde (now Lord Chancellor) was appalled when his daughter confessed the name of her lover. But when Anne asserted that James had married her secretly, in the Netherlands, the previous autumn, he was horrified: his whole career would be put in jeopardy if his daughter incurred royal wrath by setting herself up as wife to the heir to the throne.

There is much doubt as to whether the marriage was valid. Anne had no document, no reliable witnesses, to prove it. In fact, there is even evidence that she had earlier tried to induce a miscarriage, which she surely would not if she had really believed herself to be James's wife. But when her attempts at abortion had failed, she held firm to her story of the wedding.

The scandal broke that summer of 1660, and for some weeks it occupied first place in palace gossip. Hyde was trying to save his career by repudiating Anne, even, it was said, demanding that she be sent to the Tower for her temerity. The Duke of York panicked and, like many another man with his head in the marriage-trap, called up his friends to help him: one by one they came forward to claim possible paternity of Anne's baby.

Truth and motive become blurred at this point. One version of the story has King Charles insisting that his brother marry Anne; another, James's own account, has the Duke persuading a reluctant King to allow him to honour his commitment. Or it may be that the marriage was valid, and that the royal brothers found themselves forced to recognise it for fear that, if James made a regular marriage with another woman, the legitimacy of their children would always be called in doubt by this prior contract. But whatever the truth of the situation, in the end Anne Hyde won her point. On 3 September 1660 she and James were married (or 're-married'), and their son, born on the 22nd, was legitimate. He, Charles, Duke of Cambridge, died of small-pox in infancy—rather an anti-climax to the whole unfortunate business.

However, James and Anne built a happy marriage, and the new Duchess swiftly assumed such airs of dignity and regality that contemporaries were as admiring as they were amazed at her adaptability. In the years that followed, she gave birth to several children, but only two survived childhood: the Princesses Mary and Anne.

Like his elder brother, the Duke of York had become widely experienced with women during his exile, and it was not to be expected that he could be faithful to his wife for long. He was not. And, if Charles was a gourmet of women, James was a gourmand, apparently rating quantity above quality. Indeed, it was the King himself who suggested that the Duke's out-standingly plain mistresses were penances imposed on him by his priests for the good of his soul.

James himself was not unattractive: he was as fair as his brother was dark, his features more regular than Charles's, aquiline and fine drawn. He was tall and straight, graceful in his gait, more dignified than the King, though less elegant and bonhomous. But James had not Charles's natural air of enjoying life and love: he took life seriously and his pleasures so lugu-briously that Nell Gwyn named him 'dismal Jimmy'.

Like Charles too, James looked mainly to the Court to provide him with his mistresses, to the household of his wife and of the Queen. Of the many ladies-in-waiting who 'pleasured' the Duke of York, there was Jane Middleton, who resorted to the bath-tub even less than her contemporaries, so that the diarist Pepys said she carried "about her body a continual base smell, that was very offensive, especially if she were hot";[2] and Goditha Price, Lady Robartes, Elizabeth Hamilton and several others. Unlike the King, the Duke was often troubled by husbands not recognising the 'honour' which he paid to their wives by his attentions: Robartes swept his wife off to Wales, and Lord Chesterfield despatched his to their country estate in Derbyshire with such a ludicrous show of jealousy that sending one's wife 'to the Peak' became a joke throughout the Court. More serious was the Denham affair, with tragic consequences.

In 1666 the elderly Sir John Denham came upon his young wife Margaret giggling with the Duke of York over a guitar: he took the instrument from her hands and smashed it on the floor. But Lady Denham cared nothing for her husband, and by the autumn of 1666 was the ducal mistress for all to see. However, her reign did not last long: suddenly, in January 1667, she died. Inevitably, Denham himself was suspected as her murderer, and, after recent sorrows, the scandal was enough to send him insane: he accosted the King one day, claiming to be the Holy Ghost, and had to be firmly conducted out of Court.

The Duke was not so inconsolable. Within the year he had taken Arabella Churchill into his bed. She, another maid-of-honour, had apparently no attractions of feature or form until it was revealed one day, when she fell from her horse, that her legs were of incomparable shapeliness. Arabella survived in the Duke's affections—though not alone—until 1678.

Duchess Anne took her husband's infidelities in her stride. She was a strong-willed woman of acute intelligence, and she knew the exact extent of her power over the Duke. It was, indeed, said of her, that in all but his *amours* she led James by the nose. And the most potent proof of her power was her conversion of her husband to the Catholic Church, in 1668. For years in his youth he had withstood the blandishments of his mother, Henrietta Maria, who never ceased to pray that her sons might leave their Anglican 'heresy'; and even in the pre-Restoration years, when conversion would have enhanced his chances in obtaining a wealthy and prestigious bride from the Continental dynasties, James had shown no signs of 'going over to Rome'. As Charles II's heir, it was obviously to his advantage to remain an Anglican, and it is a tribute as much to his obtuseness as to his conscience that James was finally won over by his wife, who had preceded him into the Catholic fold.

The King could not dissuade the Duke from this dangerous step, but he did induce him to keep it secret for some time, so that they could continue to take Communion together under the Anglican rite, for form's sake. But in 1671, James could no longer reconcile himself with this compromise. He openly avowed his conversion. And there his troubles began—troubles which in 1688 would end with his loss of the throne. All that Charles could do was to insist that the children of the York marriage should be brought up as Protestants.

The impetus to James's public confession of faith had come from the death of his wife, that spring. He was held to his conviction by the influence of another woman, the Italian princess Maria Beatrice (known in England as Mary) of Modena whom he married in September 1673, when he was in his forties, and she only fifteen.

It was said that, enamoured as James was of this new young wife, ironically a great beauty, within a week of their wedding he had returned to Arabella. And, like Queen Catherine, Duchess Mary had to endure one miscarriage after another, while her husband's mistress gave him children: four 'Fitzjameses' were born in the years of their liaison.

But Arabella had been James's mistress long before Mary arrived in England; it was infinitely more galling to the Duchess when, in 1678, he cast off the old love and took a new one:

Catherine Sedley. And while Mary continued to miscarry, Catherine gave James another daughter.

Catherine was still annoying Mary (she did excellent imitations of her Italian priests) when James succeeded to the throne in 1685. There were rumours that she would inherit the palace apartments now vacated by the redundant Louise, Duchess of Portsmouth, but in fact James had decided to turn over a new leaf and, after creating his mistress Countess of Dorchester, at last succumbed to his wife's threats and tears and sent her packing. Catherine refused to go to Flanders, which James had suggested: she had heard it was crowded with convents, and she did not fancy being lured into one never to reappear. Instead she went to Dublin, in February 1686, her coach followed by three others crammed with her pickings. Queen Mary was seen to be more cheerful.

But the following September, Countess Catherine suddenly presented herself in the royal drawing-room. She had come back across the Irish Sea ostensibly to take the waters at Tunbridge Wells, and to try her luck. However, she never completely regained her ascendancy: James continued to frequent her house on occasion, but relations with his wife improved. Then, at last, on 10 June 1688, Queen Mary gave birth to a son.

James II was triumphant. He had a son to succeed him on the throne, and one whom he might rear as a Catholic. All around him were the ruins of his own misguided policies, but with the royal succession assured, and the danger of his crown passing to his Protestant daughters averted, he could look ahead to a better future.

The event was not viewed in the same light by the vast majority of his subjects. They had tolerated James only as a short-term monarch, and knew that whatever he did with the Church and the Constitution could be undone by his Protestant successors. But now they could envisage a future in which one Catholic Stuart king would succeed another, and the kingdom would be ruined. In the turmoil after the birth of James Francis Edward, Prince of Wales, it was even suggested that the baby was not the Queen's own, but a changeling smuggled into her bed in a warming-pan by a King desperate for a male heir, whose wife was unable to provide one.

Grave events followed swiftly. Before the summer was out, England was in the throes of revolution. In September, William,

Prince of Orange, husband of the King's elder daughter Mary, landed in the west with an army at his back—reminiscent of the Monmouth Rebellion. William said at first that he had come not to seize the throne but to promote the Protestant cause and restore English liberties, but as one politician, one general, one nobleman after another deserted the King and rode into William's camp, it became ever more obvious that James could not withstand the pressure they would put on him, and that, since everyone knew that he would never yield his principles, the end of his reign was near.

James II did not abdicate, though, in retrospect, constitutionalists tried to show that he had by desertion of his kingdom. When the danger was at its height, he despatched Queen Mary and their son to France and, while making pretence of negotiating with his son-in-law, himself departed in the last days of the year.

Four months later, William and Mary were proclaimed and crowned King and Queen.

The discarded mistress, Catherine Sedley, made no move to join James in France, but his son the Duke of Berwick (by Arabella Churchill) remained loyal to his father and half-brother throughout their struggles to regain the throne. In 1689 in Ireland, James led an army against William III, but to no avail: his troops were overwhelmingly defeated at the Boyne, and the disconsolate King sailed back to the haven of France. He remained there for the rest of his life, dying in September 1701.

It was rumoured that in his last years James still took mistresses, but there is no concrete evidence of the fact. Indeed, he became ever more gloomily devout, pouring out on paper confessions of past sins and compiling a testament intended for his son, to deter him from similar vices. The young Prince of Wales was brought up in an atmosphere of depression and hopelessness, and, succeeding to his father's title at the age of thirteen, was always weighed down with the burden of his inheritance. Charged by his father on his deathbed to cling to his faith rather than be tempted to renounce it in favour of the crown, the young man never forgot the injunction.

It is possible that, if he had been less adamant, he might have come to the throne. William and Mary died childless and were succeeded by James II's younger daughter Anne, who after numerous pregnancies, saved only one child from death in infancy—only to have him die in his early teens. Anne always harboured a measure of guilt at her desertion of her father in 1688, and would have been only too glad to adopt her half-brother as her heir, but she would never do so at the expense of the Anglican Church. Before his death, her brother-in-law King William had made arrangements that, in default of Anne's own heirs, the crown should pass to their nearest Protestant relations, the ducal family of Hanover in Germany, who were descended from the daughter of James I. It was by no means an ideal, or a wholly popular arrangement, but for want of better it had to suffice.

Queen Anne died in 1714, and, despite their qualms, the people of Britain received George of Hanover as her successor. But there remained a not-unappreciable body of opinion that the Stuart pretender, 'James III', should now be called home to reign. James's invasion force was duly mounted, his supporters called to his standard, and on 22 December 1715* he landed on the Scottish coast near Aberdeen.

Six weeks later, he was on his way back across the North Sea. The Jacobites were everywhere in retreat.

It was to be thirty years before another full-scale attempt was made to wrest the crown from the Hanoverians. Then it was James's son Charles Edward who donned the tartan and the sword, for the Old Pretender was sunk deep in his Italian lethargy.

'Bonnie Prince Charlie' the Scots called him, for his glossy and debonair charms. And charming he was in the days of his enterprise into Scotland, a romantic hero speeding through the heather, evading his captors and drawing from the hearts of men and women a courage and fortitude which owed as much to his personal magnetism as to the cause.

But in the years after his defeat and return to exile, the Prince lost both looks and amiability. And his relations with women became macabre and violent.

In his youth, the Prince had been closely guarded against the dominant Stuart sin, brought up by his intensely pious Polish mother, Maria Clementina Sobieska, to treat members of the opposite sex with an aloof chivalry. For herself, she had

---

* Old Style; New Style, 2 January 1716.

retreated into a convenient delicacy of health as soon as she found out how dreary and frustrating life with 'James III' could be, and her son was encouraged to treat her like frail porcelain. Inevitably, in manhood he revolted against early habits. He took a Polish mistress, Marie-Louise Jablonowska, Princesse de Talmond, and mistreated her cruelly—though she seems to have given as good as she got, quarrelling with him and making noisy scenes in public. She only broke with him when he transferred his brawls and beatings to one Clementina Walkinshaw, whom he had met briefly in Scotland during the '45 and who joined him in Ghent in 1752. The following year, on 29 October, Clementina bore him his only known child, whom the Prince himself carried to the font and named Charlotte.

It can only have been love which kept Clementina with Charles in the years which followed. Not for her the lavish gifts and fragrant compliments of other royal mistresses, but bruises and verbal abuse every day of her life with the Prince. The Jacobites in exile warned Charles time after time that his mistress was an English-paid spy, but out of sheer Stuart stubbornness he would not dismiss her; he did not love her, he openly asserted, but he would not be browbeaten into anything Together the couple descended into a stupor of alcoholic insensibility, only increasing each other's misery.

Then, on the night of 22 July 1760, she left him, and, with her child, found shelter in a convent. Enraged, the Prince even applied to his patron, Louis XV of France, to force Clementina to return to him, but the King, who had borne a good deal of insolence and annoyance from Charles, refused to interfere.

The Prince was fifty-one years old when at last he married, and, though his claims to the British crown were now long-since hopeless, he did so to beget an heir to keep up the tragic cause. The victim chosen by his advisers and himself was a nineteen-year-old innocent, Princess Louise of Stolberg-Gedern, who was brought out of a convent with the dazzling prospect of marrying the hero of the '45 adventure and of wearing a queen consort's crown. She was to be bitterly disappointed. She found a man old and fat, with a mottled skin and cold eyes, and her crown was an ornament with no meaning. Admitted, Charles did his best at first, moderating his drinking and paying kind attentions to his bride, but as with Clementina, he became possessive and jealous, unreasonable in his demands that the girl be gracious

to the members of his unsavoury Italian Court and then angry
when she smiled on anyone but himself. By the end of 1773
'Queen' Louise had been replaced by yet more bottles. There
was to be no child of the marriage.

In 1777 Louise found a man more appreciative of her beauty
and talents in the young Italian poet Vittorio Alfieri. At first,
the relationship remained within the bounds of conventionality
(even the most respectable noble Italian matrons had their
cavaliere servante), without any thought of adultery; but there
was enough in their intimacy to rouse Charles to outraged
reproaches. For some time, the married couple had slept apart
but, on 30 November 1780, the drunken Prince broke into
his wife's bedroom and raped her; only her cries for help and the
arrival of servants prevented his killing her, so the Princess later
asserted. Soon afterwards Louise, like Clementina before her,
disappeared into a convent.

Alfieri had undoubtedly been the prime mover in the Princess's escape, but in the first months of her freedom, while she
petitioned the Pope for protection, he remained out of sight,
letting the scandal flood by. Then, they came together again,
and for the next twenty years, until Alfieri's death in 1803,
they remained together. Louise died in 1824.

The last years of Charles Edward Stuart were happier than
he probably deserved. Deserted by Louise, he turned to his
only child, Clementina's daughter Charlotte, whom he summoned to live with him in Florence in 1784. She was by then
thirty-one years old, sufficiently strong-minded and stubborn
to curtail her father's drinking, an amusing companion who
relieved the tedium which he had always suffered so grudgingly.
On 31 January 1788 he died in his daughter's arms.

In the first months of their life together, Charles had created
Charlotte, Duchess of Albany, had drawn up a Will making her
his main heir, and had taken such steps as he could to legitimate
her. But a century had passed since Charlotte's great-grandfather
James II had been turned out by his subjects, and three decades
had gone by since her father had failed to take the throne by
force: apart from a few old men in Highland castles and crofts,
and a few eccentrics still exiled on the Continent, there was now
no Jacobite party, certainly no means of her claiming the throne
even if Charlotte had any desire to be queen, which she had not.
And in fact she died less than eleven months after her father.

9

Mrs Morley and Mrs Freeman

In terms of royal sexuality, the seventeenth century closed as ambiguously as it had opened. William III has generally been cited as a homosexual, Mary II and Anne as quasi-lesbians: in fact, when the evidence is weighed, it is not possible to be so certain about their propensities. It is true that all three were happiest in the company of their own sex, and that all found the deepest emotional response there, but there is nothing to suggest that there was an orgastic homosexuality or lesbianism in their relationships.

William III was warm and out-going, sympathetic and comradely with his male friends, cold and reserved with his wife: yet for many years he kept a mistress. Mary II and Anne, the daughters of James II, formed passionate attachments to other women, but both loved their husbands. Not even the term 'bisexual' adequately covers the enigmatic sexuality of these three monarchs.

Today, perhaps, we are too ready to read sexuality into relationships where there is only emotion. To deny that there were sexual relationships between William III and Bentinck or Keppel, Mary II and Frances Apsley, Queen Anne and Sarah Churchill, is not to be as naïve as Queen Victoria who, when shown a parliamentary bill condemning homosexual partnerships, refused to believe that they could exist between women: it is only to deny sexual 'perversion' in three specific cases.

Since the revelations of the psychologist Sigmund Freud, we have become accustomed to seeking the causes of abnormal sexual tendencies in childhood experience. It would certainly be interesting to know what his analysis would be of the traumas of royal children of the past. Until the nineteenth century, they were rarely brought up by, or even in close proximity to, their parents. From an early age, they were in the care of guardians and servants, occupying their own houses, maintaining their own staff. Parents might be affectionate, but they would not be as emotionally close to their children as is considered the norm today: a royal baby would be suckled by a wet-nurse, its intimate physical needs attended to by various servants, so that the mother-child bond was never strongly forged; and relations between fathers and their children were usually of the most formal.

Nevertheless, even the most distant parents would be a focus for a child's affections and provide a stability which would help its emotional development. Mary and Anne, the daughters of James II by his first wife, Anne Hyde, had not even this anchor. Mary, the elder, was sent off at an early age to live with her maternal grandparents, the Hydes, only to have her grandmother die when she was three years old; Anne, at four, was despatched to France, to have specialist eye-treatment, under the care of their other grandmother, Henrietta Maria: the dowager Queen died a few months after the child's arrival, and she was passed on to her aunt 'Minette', Duchess of Orleans, who was also dead within a year. Anne had not long been home when she and Mary lost their mother, Anne Hyde. Nor could the Princesses' stepmother fill the void: when James announced his marriage to his daughters, he told them that he was bringing them not a new mother but a play-fellow, for Mary of Modena was only fifteen years old when she arrived in England in 1673.

Throughout history, royal children frequently formed enduring attachments to their parent-substitutes, usually their nurses or governesses: Edward VI had his 'Mother Jak', and his half-sister Elizabeth—a prime example of deprived childhood—was brought up by her governess Catherine Ashley, who remained her confidante until death parted them; and she kept in her entourage one Blanche Parry, who had originally been her 'cradle-rocker'. Under different circumstances, the future Queen Victoria would cling to her governess, Louise Lehzen, into adulthood—with almost disastrous consequences for her marriage, when her husband, Albert, found cause to be jealous of their exclusive intimacy.

The detachment of royal children, especially princesses, from their parents, may have been in part deliberate, for so many of them were destined to leave home and family in their early teens, to go to foreign countries to be married and perhaps never to

Barbara Villiers (Lady Castle-maine, Duchess of Cleveland), mistress of Charles II in the 1660s and mother of five of his children.

Louise de Keroualle, the French maid-of-honour who became Charles II's mistress in 1671 and whom he created Duchess of Portsmouth.

'Sweet Nell of Old Drury', the Cockney barmaid, orange-seller and comic actress who was admitted to Charles II's harem in about 1669. (Nell Gwyn and her son the Duke of St Albans: by Sir Peter Lely.)

Arabella Churchill—it was reputedly her fine legs which attracted the future King James II to her. (Portrait in the Green Writing-Room, Blenheim Palace.)

see their homeland again. Often they were even required to leave behind them their friends and servants, not permitted to carry into their new homes any reminder of rival loyalties—there is a letter extant containing a pitiful plea from Henry VIII's younger sister Mary to be allowed to keep her old governess, whom she calls 'Mother Guilford', when the Princess was sent off to France to marry King Louis XII.

There is little evidence that Mary and Anne found any such parent-substitutes: Mary seems to have been devoted to her nurse Mrs Langford (whom she calls 'my Mam'), but certainly not to have found her a total compensation for other losses. The governess provided for the motherless Princesses was Lady Frances Villiers, who, with her husband, was awarded the lease of Richmond Palace, where they brought up the two girls among their own daughters and several other girl-companions. But there was a boarding-school atmosphere at Richmond, and, though Mary and Anne were undoubtedly the most important members of the establishment, there is not the slightest evidence that they were especially cosseted by their guardians.

However, as in other single-sex boarding-schools, passionate attachments between the inmates did build up, with an intensity which would today be considered unhealthy. Allowed only occasional excursions into the fairyland of their uncle Charles II's Court, the two girls were trapped in the emotional hothouse of Richmond. It was inevitable that they should expend their affections on the only available objects.

When the future King James II committed his thoughts on education to paper, he wisely ordained that, "You as have young persons under your charge, should not let them read romances, more especially the womenkind, 'tis but loss of time and is apt to put foolish and ridiculous thoughts into their heads."[1] He was speaking from experience, from the discovery of his own daughters' follies.

It was, of course, inevitable, that the girls should find vicarious excitement in the romances (the forerunners of the modern novel), poetry and drama which was the bulk of their reading-matter, and that they should transfer them into their own prosaic lives. When Mary, at about the age of twelve, began her correspondence with a former inmate of Richmond, twenty-year-old Frances Apsley, the two girls adopted the names of characters in contemporary plays: 'Clorine' and 'Aurelia' respectively—and the language which Mary at least employed (only one of Frances's letters survives) was the language of the romantic heroine, full of sighs and 'alas', of recriminations for supposed slights and cruelties, vain yearnings for the loved one's presence.

It is frustrating that Frances Apsley's letters to Mary do not survive, for from them one might be able to deduce more firmly if the Princess led or followed in the relationship, if she was the one who loved or the one who allowed herself to be loved. From what is known, the former is more likely, though Mary chose the submissive role and, even as she addressed Frances as 'Aurelia', might in the same sentence name her as her 'husband'.

Nothing could be more passionate than Mary's letters to Frances, addressed to her "dear dear dear dear dear dear Aurelia":

I may, if I can, tell you how much I love you, but I hope that is not doubted. I have given you proofs enough. If not, I will die to satisfy you, dear, dear, husband. If all my hairs were lives, I would lose them all twenty times over to serve or satisfy you . . . I love you with a flame more lasting than the vestals' fire. Thou art my life, my soul, my all that Heaven can give. Death's life with you, without you death to live. What more can I say to persuade you that I love you with more zeal than any lover can. I love you with a love that never was known by man. I have for you excess of friendship more of love than any woman can for woman, and more love than ever the constantest lover had for his mistress. You are loved more than can be expressed by your ever obedient wife, very affectionate friend, humble servant, to kiss the ground where you go, to be your dog on a string, your fish in a net, your bird in a cage, your humble trout,

Mary Clorine[2]

Any modern parent would say that such unchildlike emotion was unhealthy: Lady Frances Villiers seemed to think so, for Mary found it necessary to conceal from her that she was corresponding in this manner with Frances Apsley after the latter had left Richmond. When the younger Princess, Anne, was found to be conducting a similarly absurd intercourse with a Miss Cecily Cornwallis, her father was appalled by the expression of sentiments and forbade it to continue.

Before long, in 1676, Anne was Mary's rival for Frances Apsley's time and ink. Where Mary and Frances were 'Clorine' and 'Aurelia', Anne and Frances were 'Ziphares' and 'Semandra', roles which they had taken in Nathaniel Lee's play *Mithradate*. Mary, inevitably, was jealous.

Soon, however, she was left to enjoy her 'husband' in peace, for Anne had taken up with a far more accessible girl, another Richmond companion, Sarah Jennings, whose love she did not, as yet, have to share with anyone.

Where Anne was plump, stolid and slow, Sarah was all quicksilver. Six years the Princess's senior, she was always to be the dominant partner, though undoubtedly Anne herself made the running in passionate avowals: Sarah, shrewdly aware of the possibilities for her career of being 'all in all' to the Princess, would have been happier with less sentimentality. In about 1678 (the exact date is not known) Sarah married John Churchill, brother of the Duke of York's mistress Arabella (and distant cousin and one-time lover of Barbara Villiers, Duchess of Cleveland). In her life with Churchill she found perfect fulfilment and happiness, and her assiduous attentions to Anne then, and in more than three decades afterwards, were performed as much with an eye to her John's advancement as to her own.

To return to Princess Mary: in 1677 her marriage to her cousin William of Orange was arranged. The match was of her uncle's making, in response to political exigencies which demanded an alliance with the Netherlands. And William, as son of Charles's sister Mary, next in line of succession to the throne after his York cousins, was a fit partner. He was also, like Mary, a Protestant, and Charles was eager to have his niece married before her father could persuade him to give her a Catholic husband.

Mary wept piteously when she heard the plan for her future. Nothing could comfort her for the loss of home and country— and Frances Apsley. When her stepmother reminded Mary that she had left her own family to marry the Duke and had yet found happiness, the Princess sobbed out, "But you were *coming* to England!"

It was an incongruous couple who stood together before the temporary altar erected in Mary's apartments at St. James's Palace on 4 November 1677. The bridegroom was twenty-seven years old, the bride fifteen. William was just over five feet six inches tall, Mary five feet eleven. He was frail and sallow, she statuesque and brilliantly complexioned. He stood taut and impassive; she was racked with tears.

Princess Anne was not at her sister's wedding. She was suffering from a mild attack of smallpox, and her doctors so feared to increase her fever with the emotion of the parting that it was not until Mary had left for her new home in Holland that the news was broken to her younger sister.

The smallpox had also deprived Mary of the comfort of having her governess with her. Lady Frances Villiers had been named as the leader of the Princess's entourage which was to go with her when she left England, but she became ill at the same time as Anne, and died just as Mary embarked for the Continent. Others among the Princess's Richmond companions went with her, but not Frances Apsley, and the letters which Mary wrote now are made confusing by her references to her 'husbands', the old and the new.

Though the young Princess of Orange had refused to believe that she could ever be happy again, soon she found that her new life was extremely pleasant. The cool, light Dutch palaces compared favourably with the musty, frowzy, squalid grandeur of St James's, and Dutch hygiene and order were just to Mary's taste. The Dutch ladies were welcoming, and the Princess soon struck up friendships with them—though most of her attendants were English. She enjoyed, too, being the undisputed leader of fashion. Above all, she fell in love with her husband.

Mary had known few men. She was, after all, only fifteen years old and had rarely been outside the Richmond circle or that of her stepmother's ladies before her wedding. How she might have fared with a bridegroom nearer her own age, and more sympathetic, must ever be a matter for conjecture: the only man to whom she was closely attached, apart from William, was her cousin the Duke of Monmouth—and he was a year older than her husband.

William of Orange had been through a hard school by the time he married Mary of York, and was a prime example of the old head on young shoulders.

The posthumous son of William II of Orange, he was brought up by his mother, the English Princess Royal, until her death when he was only ten years old. Formerly the House of Orange had ruled the United Provinces of the Netherlands almost as their personal kingdom (at least, so their enemies said): after the death of William II, the Republican party gained the ascendancy and for years it seemed unlikely that the Prince would ever be elected to the power which his forefathers had enjoyed. When he entered politics, in his teens, it was to attempt the overthrow of the Grand Pensionary de Witt—only to fail. War, however, accomplished what political manœuvring could not: with the Dutch overwhelmingly defeated by the French in 1672, the mob lynched de Witt (whom they held responsible for their humiliation), leaving William, now Stadholder of most of the states and Captain General of the Army, as leader of the nation—he was still only twenty-two years old.

The war with France was to continue for decades, but William's armies began to turn the tide. It was in hopes of gaining England as an ally, with her army and navy to help him against France, that the Prince came to his English marriage. He was not to know that his Uncle Charles, a crypto-Catholic in the pay of Louis XIV, was so closely pledged to France that he would do nothing to help his nephew, and that his new father-in-law, while professing approbation of the match, was even then writing to the King of France and the Pope to apologise for allowing the wedding.

The Prince of Orange always treated his wife with the utmost courtesy and consideration, but she was always to mourn that he never shared his inmost thoughts with her. Her rival, his confidant, was Hans Willem Bentinck, once his page, now his closest adviser. Bentinck had, indeed—or so William always believed—saved his life when, some years earlier, he had succumbed to smallpox: Bentinck had slept in the Prince's bed, "drawing the fever into himself", so the doctors would have it. It was a risk and a sacrifice which William never forgot.

That William was homosexual and Bentinck his partner has often been asserted, despite lack of evidence. The Prince was always at his best in male company, losing his staid reserve with fellow-soldiers and courtiers, and in later life he would be attracted by young men as bright, amusing and good-looking as the minions of James I: but there is no real evidence of William's 'perversion' beyond one reproof by the contemporary Bishop Burnet that "he had no vice but of one sort, in which he was very cautious and secret",[3] a comment which might just as well refer to the Prince's secretive liaison with Betty Villiers as to anything else.

Certainly, both Bentinck and his successor Arnoud Joost van Keppel proved themselves heterosexual: the former married twice, the latter was a notorious womaniser. And, while Mary is known to have suffered agonies over her husband's involvement with Betty Villiers, there is no hint in any of her writings that she suspected him of other attachments. Pious and conformist, Mary would have been infinitely more horrified by homosexuality than by heterosexual licence.

Even as the Princess fell in love with her husband, she was still corresponding with Frances Apsley, but her fervour and her complaints at their parting became less as the months passed, and she could joke about their past relations when she could at last announce to her 'husband' that she was pregnant: "I have played the whore a little; because the sea parts us, you may believe that it is a bastard."[4] But one miscarriage followed another and, after a serious illness, Mary was told that she would never have children.

This great sadness was deepened by her discovery, almost immediately afterwards, that her husband was having an *affaire* with one of her English ladies. Mary probably learned of this, which may have been a successful secret for some years, in the spring of 1680, not by her own observation but through the meddling of her friends. Yet, seemingly, for five years, she kept the pain to herself. Her letters to Frances Apsley resume their tone of passion, and the Princess becomes more demanding, fierce in her complaints when a letter from England is overdue, but not once does she unburden herself to her confidante.

William's secret mistress, Elizabeth Villiers, was one of Mary's childhood playmates at Richmond—though never one of her close intimates. 'Betty' Villiers was no beauty: she had a squint, and in face and figure in no way compared with the ripe, Junoesque Mary whom everyone admired. What attracted William to her must remain a mystery. Perhaps he came to her because his friend Bentinck had married her sister Anne, though the two sisters were not alike in personality: Anne Bentinck was as docile, obedient, affectionate a wife as was Mary herself; Betty was a wit, and reputedly had a sharp independence.

Only in 1685 did husband and wife come to admit the situation. Mary's earlier informers, her maid-of-honour Anne Trelawney and her nurse ('my Mam') Mrs Langford, goaded her into charging William with his infidelity at last. They had their own reasons: both were spies in the Orange household, paid by Mary's father, now King of England.

One night the Prince emerged from his mistress's room to find his wife shivering on the stairs below, lying in wait for him. They quarrelled. William stormed; Mary wept.

When William revealed all to Bentinck, the latter had no sympathy for him. He spoke harshly of his sister-in-law (and later forbade his wife to receive Betty), urging William to fidelity to Mary. For the first time, the two friends quarrelled.

What happened next rests on the most slenderly accreditable authority. Daniel de Bourdon, an unreliable source, avers that William went to Mary and declared that he was not guilty of adultery: she believed him and they were reconciled. However, it is certain that Anne Trelawney and Mrs Langford and her husband were immediately dismissed and sent back to England, not allowed to see or communicate with Mary before they left. And—likely evidence that the Princess still believed her husband guilty—at this point she tried her strength against her rival. In William's absence, she sent for Betty Villiers and charged her to carry a letter to England, to James II. The woman was still in the Princess's employ and could not refuse. Nevertheless, having crossed the Channel, she opened the letter and found it to contain Mary's urgent plea to her father to detain her in England. Of course Betty did not take the letter to the King: instead, she showed it to her own father, who advised her to return to Holland without delay.

When she entered the palace, Mary refused to see her. Bentinck tried to persuade her to leave. She would not. Soon, however, William heard of the whole trick, and Betty was swiftly re-established among his wife's ladies.

Mary came to accept the situation. Betty Villiers continued in her household all through the Oranges' last years in the Netherlands: when Mary went to England, in 1689, Betty went too. The Princess's recovery from the shock cannot be charted by any definite word of her own: the main evidence is in the cooling of her tone in writing to Frances (now Lady Bathurst). As in the early days of her happiness, Mary is now remiss in her correspondence, and what letters there are are full of apologies for the long space between them. She no longer needed this prop to her loneliness.

In 1688 William of Orange embarked his army for England,

to overthrow the rule of James II, with the full approval of the King's daughter. Mary was convinced that the son born to James by his second wife was a changeling: during Mary of Modena's pregnancy, the Princess of Orange had set her sister Anne to watch and, if possible, to find out if their stepmother was deceiving them and the nation: but Anne was not present at the Queen's confinement, and neither she nor Mary would believe that the alleged Prince of Wales was truly their half-brother. Considerations of James's bad government apart, Mary of Orange had no wish to see herself, and her husband, supplanted in the royal line of succession by a half-brother whom James II would certainly use to ensure the Catholic succession of the crown.

William went to England—England welcomed him—James fled. After Parliament had debated the terms on which the succession should pass to William and Mary—as joint sovereigns, an unprecedented situation, the couple agreed to abide by the nation's restraints on their powers. They were crowned together on 11 April 1689.

Betty Villiers remained at Court to serve William and Mary in different ways, but she was never the King's *maîtresse-en-titre* as her predecessors of Charles II's reign had been. If anything may be said for her conduct, it is that she was supremely discreet. There were sly sniggers from the courtiers, the remnants of the rakes and belles of the Merry Monarch's coterie, but never an open scandal.

In 1694 Queen Mary II died. Now at last, the King realised her worth and, too late, loved her. He mourned her as sincerely and as openly as if they had been Darby and Joan.

In penitence, he gave up Elizabeth Villiers. She was pensioned off with grants of land worth £30,000 a year and, in November 1695, married Lord George Hamilton, who was created Earl of Orkney. William continued to meet his former mistress only in public: she became one of the capital's foremost hostesses and, after her many years of obscurity, won fame for her lively mind.

Nowhere is there any evidence of Betty Villiers' own feelings for William. Perhaps, since for so long she had been content to remain in the shadows, she genuinely loved him; apparently she needed no material rewards to keep her faithful. That she had political influence over the King is eminently unlikely. Only once is she seen to be involved in his designs, and then only as his agent: William employed her to attempt to persuade a recalcitrant politician, the Duke of Shrewsbury, to enter his government—and even then, she failed.

'Squinting Betty', as her contemporaries called her, was one of the most discreet of royal mistresses, undemanding, childless and apparently faithful. She must surely have felt insulted when, many years later, in the drawing-room of King George II, she met Louise de Kergualle and Catherine Sedley, who had few of her qualities, and was associated with them in Catherine Sedley's exclamation, "Who would have thought that we three whores should meet here!"

In fact, so discreet had the King been in his relations with Elizabeth Villiers that those who began to suspect him of homosexual leanings, during his years in England, had no idea of this 'proof' of heterosexuality. They saw only that William was openly affectionate to a handsome Dutch page, several years his junior, training his new favourite, as James I had with Carr, for the post of his own secretary and awarding him the titles and honours usually accorded to royal paramours of either sex.

This was Arnoud Joost van Keppel, one of the many Dutchmen whom William had brought over to England. Plump and rather pretty-faced, the young man had all the traits of pride and vanity which had been so reviled in James I's favourites and, though he had a sharp intelligence, he had little learning or solid training to fit him for a place in government. Hitherto, that is until the mid 1690s, Bentinck had been William's closest confidant in government matters, and he was bitterly resentful of so unworthy a rival.

It was Bentinck who, in fact, told the King of the gossip about his relations with Keppel—gossip which had reached back even to Holland—warning him of the suspicions against

the kindness which Your Majesty has for this young man and the manner in which you seem to authorise those liberties and that insolence which make people say things which I am ashamed to hear and from which I think you as far as any man in the world. I thought it was only the malicious in England who had invented those bloody things, but I was thunderstruck when I saw that The Hague and the army were full of the same talk.

William could only reply that, "It is a most extraordinary thing that one could have no esteem or friendship for a young man without its being criminal."[5] (Certainly this does not appear to be the language which two former homosexual partners would use in discussing the 'infidelity' of one of them.)

Nevertheless, the King gave his old friend cause to be jealous of the trust and honours he awarded to Keppel. Bentinck he had created Earl of Portland as a tribute to and reward for long years of service, but now he created the untried Keppel Earl of Albemarle and made him the channel for political and Court advancement. Bentinck at one point threatened a breach with the King, but the flash-point was avoided and, though he spent long periods away from Court after Keppel's rise, he never wholly forfeited William's trust.

Both men were with the King in 1702 when he lay dying. He had had a fall while hunting (Jacobites toasted the "little gentleman in the black velvet waistcoat"—the mole in whose hole the King's horse had stumbled, throwing him'), and his always frail constitution could not withstand the shock. He died on 9 March 1702.

We left Queen Mary's sister Anne at Richmond, in the 1670s, falling under the spell of Sarah Jennings.

Anne had neither Mary's beauty nor much of her good sense, only her propensity for infatuation with members of her own sex. She was more fortunate than Mary, first in being allowed to remain in her own country after marrying a foreign prince, also in having a husband who never once gave her cause for concern. He, Prince George of Denmark, had had no role allotted to him in Scandinavian government and was sent (like any princess-bride) merely to breed in and to adorn England. A slow, stolid, dull man, he was the ideal mate for Anne. He chafed to render real service to his adoptive country, but everyone recognised his lack of talent in every sphere (even his own wife, who was generally no judge of character), and he lived out his life in idleness. Prince George sired more than a dozen children: it was not his fault that they died in infancy (except one, William, who survived into his early teens).

Ideal George may have been, as Anne's complement, but he might have been of more value had he been able to moderate her affections for the women to whom she gave her love and trust.

Sarah Jennings took her place in Anne's household when the

Princess married. Thereafter, though for the next few years she was frequently pregnant, she was rarely away from Anne's side. When, in 1688, it seemed likely that James II would take his daughter and son-in-law into custody, to prevent their joining William of Orange, it was Sarah who hustled Anne away to safety by night, and Sarah's husband, John Churchill, who took George of Denmark into William's camp.

For this service, William and Mary were duly grateful. In the dispensation of coronation honours, Churchill became Earl of Marlborough. However, as time passed, their gratitude cooled; Marlborough was several times suspected of Jacobite sympathies, corresponding with his nephew the Duke of Berwick, James II's son by the Earl's sister Arabella, who was with the former King in France. At the same time, the King and Queen could not but resent Anne's confidence in Lady Marlborough, who, they believed, was responsible for alienating the Princess's loyalty from them.

When Mary demanded that Sarah be dismissed from Anne's household, in 1692, the Princess refused to give her up. She took her to Court with her, defying the convention that no wife of a disgraced officer should be presented (Marlborough had recently been deprived of his command by William for alleged complicity in a plot against him). Sarah herself suggested that it might be best if she withdrew, but Anne would not hear of it:

I beg it again [she wrote] for Jesus Christ's sake, that you would never name it any more to me, for be assured, if you should ever do so cruel a thing as to leave me, from that moment I shall never enjoy one quiet hour. And should you do it without asking my consent (which if I ever give you, may I never see the face of Heaven), I will shut myself up and never see the world more, but live where I may be forgotten by human kind.[6]

By that time, Queen Mary could not sympathise with her sister in her attachment. She had long since terminated her own close relations with Frances Apsley: Frances, now Lady Bathurst, was even regarded more as one of Anne's friends by this time, since her husband was treasurer of the Princess's household.* The Queen was not sufficiently imaginative to put

---

* In fact, Bathurst betrayed his trust and was discovered in cheating the Princess in a matter of underweight coins. Soon, Frances was being named 'the Nag's head' in the Anne/Sarah letters.

herself in her sister's place and wonder how she might herself react if such a friend were threatened.

The letters from Anne to Sarah Churchill certainly demonstrate that the Princess was no less ardent in her devotion than Mary had once been to Frances Apsley. But Anne, no romantic teenager by now, had less excuse for her indulgence. The only restraint on her was their comparative ranks, and this the Princess dealt with in a characteristic manner: she proposed that the two women should address each other by pseudonyms, one 'Mrs Morley', the other 'Mrs Freeman'. "My frank, open temper naturally led me to pitch upon Freeman,"[7] recalled Sarah in later years.

She also recorded (writing of herself in the third person) that:

. . . they were shut up together for many hours daily. Every moment of absence she [Anne] counted a sort of tedious lifeless state. To see [Sarah] was a constant joy, and to part with her for never so short a time a constant uneasiness, as the Princess's own frequent expressions were. This worked even to the jealousy of her lover. She used to say she desired to possess her wholly and could hardly bear that she should ever escape from this confinement into any other company.

All who knew the tempers of them both knew it to be a great confinement indeed for one who had a very great sprightliness and cheerfulness of nature joined with a true taste of conversation, to be perpetually chained, as it were, to a person whose other accomplishments had not cured the sullenness of her temper nor wholly freed her conversation from an insipid heaviness. . . .

[Sarah] had too great a sense of her favour not to submit to all such inconveniences to oblige one who she saw loved her to excess. . . . But though there was this passionate love on the one side and, as I verily believe, the sincerest friendship on the other, yet their tempers were not more different than their principles and notions on many occasions appeared to be.[8]

When, in 1702, Anne at last succeeded her brother-in-law on the throne, all 'Mrs Freeman's' patient attentions were rewarded. She became the Queen's Mistress of the Robes, the main dispenser of royal patronage at Court and, without exaggeration, the 'power behind the throne' in politics.

John Churchill was undoubtedly one of the finest military commanders ever to draw sword for Britain (even William III had come to admit and rely on his prowess towards the end of his reign), but he needed the backing of Crown and Parliament to keep his armies in the field against those of France. For years Sarah held Anne true to the policies of 'Mr Freeman', and loyal to Marlborough's friend 'Mr Montgomery', Sidney Godolphin, who managed Parliament. Together, this triumvirate ruled Queen and country for some six or seven years.

Marlborough repaid Anne's trust. He gave Britain great victories on the Continent: Blenheim, Ramillies, Oudenarde and Malplaquet. It was after the Battle of Blenheim, in 1704, that the Queen created him Duke of Marlborough and offered to pay for the construction of a ducal palace on the royal estate at Woodstock. And now it was as 'Duchess Zarah' that Sarah Churchill was hailed by her enemies—of whom there was a great number.

Anne would not admit, in Sarah's heyday, that her friend was overbearing and often rude to her. The most she complained of was the Duchess's frequent absences from Court. True, Anne had little love for the Whig party which composed the majority of her Council, and whom John and Sarah favoured as the main supporters of the war on the Continent, but Sarah could bring the Queen to recognise them as her loyal subjects, while reminding her of the supposed Jacobite sympathies of the Tories.

In the end, Sarah herself was responsible for her own downfall. Too often she snubbed and thwarted Anne, bringing out in her that streak of unreasoning stubbornness so characteristic of the unimaginative. More immediately, however, there was the problem of the Duchess's absences from royal attendance: as a means to gain her own freedom, Sarah had introduced her daughters into the household as maids-of-honour and, in an unhappy moment, had admitted her cousin Abigail Hill as a Woman of the Bedchamber—a menial rank, but one which involved constant personal ministrations to the Queen's comfort.

Abigail Hill had good reason to be grateful to her patron, both for her post and for Sarah's having nursed her through a serious illness, but, cherishing her own ambitions, the Duchess's favours were soon forgotten. However, apart from her blatant self-interest, the woman remains an enigma. One contemporary, the author Swift, wrote of her that she "was a person of a plain, sound understanding, of great truth and sincerity, without the least mixture of falsehood or disguise, of an honest boldness and courage superior to her sex, firm and disinterested in her friendship and full of love, duty and veneration for the Queen her mistress. . . ."[9] Another, the Earl of Dartmouth, averred that Abigail was "exceeding mean and vulgar in her manners, of a very unequal temper, childishly exceptious and passionate. . . ."[10] There can be no doubt as to which opinion Sarah Churchill came to share.

Insidiously, Abigail crept into Anne's affections, with her gentle hands which could soothe a tired brow and her whispering voice which never jarred the royal nerves as did Sarah's strident carping.

The Duchess did not realise what was happening until the summer of 1707 when she heard rumours that her cousin was secretly married. Still kindly disposed towards Abigail, she offered to break the news to the Queen on her behalf. Anne already knew, said Abigail, now Mrs Masham. When the Queen herself was approached by Sarah, all she would say was "I have a hundred times bid Masham tell it you, and she would not".[11] Suspicious now, it did not take Sarah long to find out that "my cousin was an absolute favourite; that the Queen herself was present at her marriage . . .; that Mrs Masham came often to the Queen, when the Prince was asleep, and was generally two hours every day in private with her. . . ."[12]

She also found out that Abigail was using her new influence to advance the fortunes of one Robert Harley, another of her cousins, a one-time ally of Marlborough and Godolphin who, though still professing loyalty to them, was resolved to break the Whigs' power. Abigail was supplying Harley with information and, at the same time, counteracting Sarah's antipathy to him by speaking to Anne of his great loyalty to her interests.

In the months that followed, relations between the Queen and the Duchess went from bad to worse. Sarah keenly felt the ingratitude of her cousin and her friend, and neither was left in any doubt of it. There were several small contretemps between Mesdames Morley and Freeman—as when Anne did not wear the jewels which Sarah had selected her, at the thanksgiving service of August 1708 for Marlborough's victory at Oudenarde: Sarah reproached the Queen loudly for all to hear, on the very steps of St Paul's.

Then, that October, Prince George died. Sarah took charge of the weeping Anne, trying to rally her from her grief, but since she could not think the royal consort much loss, she soon lost patience with the Queen's lamentations: the Duchess even referred to the beloved's body as "that dreary corpse". All Anne wanted was to be left alone with Abigail, who was all concern.

By October 1709 relations between the two women had so far deteriorated that Anne was writing to the Duke of Marlborough that,

> I do not love complaining, but it is impossible to help saying on this occasion I believe nobody was ever so used by a friend as I have been by her ever since my coming to the crown. I desire nothing but that she would leave off teasing and tormenting me and behave herself with the decency she ought both to her friend and queen, and this I hope you will make her do.[13]

A few weeks later, Anne was refusing to discuss the situation with Sarah, and would not listen to the Duchess's pleas for a hearing. Political developments went hand in hand with the personal, and Marlborough could feel the ground being cut away from under him—with Harley wielding the shovel.

On 17 January 1711 Anne listened to Marlborough's reasonable assessment of the situation, but would not admit any mitigation for Sarah's conduct. She demanded the Duchess's gold key of office.

From then on, Anne's reign belonged to Abigail. Marlborough and Godolphin were replaced by Harley, the Whigs by the Tories. Sarah, blustering and raging, retired, to quarrel with the architect of Blenheim and with her children—with everyone, so it seems, except her John. He died in 1722, she in 1744, thirty years after Anne and ten years after Lady Masham.

The fact that Anne and Sarah's relationship ended in a welter of recriminations and bitterness cannot detract from their closeness of earlier years. It may seem that Anne did all the giving, Sarah all the taking, but that was not the whole truth. Sarah gave Anne support when she most needed it and, on the whole, wise counsel. By her own profession, she

> always endeavoured to give her notions of loving her country, of justice and governing by law and making herself to be beloved rather than feared, and I always showed her how easy that was to do when she had so much in her power to do good; and I ever told her that nothing was so great and honourable as to govern upon

Arnoud Joost van Keppel, Earl of Albermarle, a 'favourite' of King William III and possibly his partner in a homosexual relationship.

Elizabeth Villiers, Countess of Orkney—the lady-in-waiting who conducted a discreet affaire with William of Orange over a number of years.

Clementina Walkinshaw, the long-suffering mistress of 'Bonnie Prince Charlie' and mother of his daughter Charlotte.

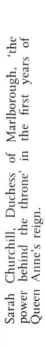

Sarah Churchill, Duchess of Marlborough, 'the power behind the throne' in the first years of Queen Anne's reign.

The Maypole and the Elephant

Queen Anne died in 1714 and, as long-since arranged, was succeeded on the throne by her distant cousin George, Elector of Hanover. It was a sure indication that Britain had no desire for another Stuart monarch that the German was accepted so readily, that the Old Pretender's challenge for the throne was so little supported in 1715.

However, though the principle of the Protestant succession was generally applauded, King George I himself was never popular in his kingdom. He arrived with a large entourage of German courtiers and ministers, immediately and always loathed by Englishmen, who harked back to the days when the first James Stuart had come south to his throne with his hordes of rapacious Scots.

"Good pipple," cried one of George's German mistresses to a mob which surrounded her carriage, shouting threats, "what for you abuse us? We come for all your goots!"

"Yes, damn ye," came the reply, "and for all our chattels too!"

The fickle populace might have been won over had they been able to spot a pretty face among the ladies who accompanied George: but they were unrelievedly frightful. The memoirist Horace Walpole, as a child, was introduced to one royal mistress, Madame von Kielmansegge, and could never forget "being terrified of her enormous figure, the fierce black eyes, large and rolling beneath two lofty arched eyebrows, two acres of cheeks spread with crimson, an ocean of neck that overflowed and was not distinguished from the lower part of her body, and no part of it retained by stays".[1] Sophia Charlotte, Baroness Kielmansegge, was named 'the elephant' by Court wits, while her elderly rival (in the friendliest way), Ehrengard Melusine von der Schulenberg, was so tall and so thin that she was dubbed 'the maypole'.

One new aspect of royal concubinage was that the Hanoverians were unashamedly incestuous. George I's father, the Elector Ernest Augustus, had been the lover of (among many others) two sisters, Clara and Maria von Meisenbuch. The former, as Countess von Platen, lived with him for many years (sharing with her husband control of the Elector's money and affairs) and gave him children. George shared Maria with his father for some time and, later, took as his mistress Clara's daughter (his own half-sister), Baroness Kielmansegge, and her daughter-in-law, another Countess von Platen (wife of his half-brother). The younger Countess, the only beauty in George's harem, remained in Hanover when he left for England accompanied by his sister-mistress van Kielmansegge and Madame von der Schulenberg.

There was no queen consort. George had been wed as a young man to his cousin Sophia Dorothea of Celle, but had divorced her. While George, in Hanover, had forgone none of the fashionable debaucheries on his own account, he would not allow his wife the same latitude—not even one consoling adultery.

The marriage had been unhappy from the start. The cousins had, of course, not chosen each other (their fathers had made the match, to unite their duchies in their descendants), but George and Sophia Dorothea came together with worse chances of future happiness than most: he was devoted to warfare and mature, *complaisante* women; she was young and ardent, romantic and emotional, so appalled by the prospect of her loveless marriage that she went into hysterics when she learned of her father's plans. In a sophisticated Court such as that of France, where neglected wives were expected to find outlets in *amours* or the arts or intrigue, Sophia Dorothea might have come to maturity without hazarding herself, but in provincial Hanover, dedicated to militarism and gourmandising, she became increasingly isolated and desperate. When the handsome Swedish Count Philip von Königsmarck appeared, Sophia Dorothea seized her chance for fulfilment and plunged into a love affair as indiscreet as it was passionate.

Königsmarck was equally enamoured of the Princess, and it was not long before he had taken pleasures which should have been guarded for Prince George. After one night of love, he wrote to his mistress: "I slept like a king, and I hope you did the same. What joy! what rapture! what enchantment have I not tasted in your sweet arms! Ye gods! what a night I spent!"[2]

It was unfortunate that, to come to Sophia Dorothea, the Count had had to free himself from the toils of a former mistress—none other than the Countess von Platen. And this woman, ruled by *amour-propre*, could not forgive him. It cannot be certainly proved, but it seems eminently likely, that it was she who forged a note in the Princess's handwriting which lured Königsmarck to Sophia Dorothea's bedchamber on the night of 1 July 1694. There he was surprised by an armed guard, arrested and borne off to a prison from which he never emerged. Or it may be, as contemporary rumour had it, that his captors strangled Königsmarck on the spot and buried him under the floor in the Princess's apartments. Certainly, he was never seen again.

If Sophia Dorothea was forced to bear the macabre presence of her former lover beneath her feet, she was not long to endure it. Prince George arranged a divorce, and she was sent, under guard, to imprisonment at the castle of Ahlden. When George went to England, in 1714, she was still there, dying only in November 1726, just seven months before her husband.

As predicted at the outset of George I's reign, the King's mistresses made themselves thoroughly at home in England, bejewelled, landed, pensioned and, like their predecessors of earlier reigns, awarded titles: Schulenberg, the senior, became Duchess of Munster in the Irish peerage in 1716 and Duchess of Kendal three years later; Kielmansegge had to content herself with the lesser title of Countess of Darlington. However, they never directly influenced their royal lover in politics, as many had feared, though their favour was always a channel to Court office, bought dearly (Schulenberg "would have sold the King's honour for a shilling advance to the best bidder", it was said[3]).

'The maypole' and 'the elephant' amicably divided the honours of George I's bed, and only in the last years of his life did he favour an Englishwoman with his attentions: but she, Anne Brett, was a nonentity who never seriously rivalled her elders from Hanover. Indeed, the kingdom of Great Britain was no rival to Hanover itself: George made no pretence of enjoying anything but British gold, which was freely disbursed for the benefit of his German duchy, and as often as he could be spared, he made his way home for long visits.

The King was, in fact, on his way to Hanover when he died, in June 1727. After a heavy meal the previous evening, he had endured much discomfort, and on the road he suffered an apoplectic fit. His surgeon was at hand, but there was nothing he could do to save George. He died that night.

In later years, there was a strange story told of Madame Schulenberg, Duchess of Kendal. It was said that she kept a raven, which she believed to be King George reincarnated: she cared for it tenderly until she died.

George I's son, another George, had a finer taste in feminine charms than his father's, and English and German women shared his favours evenly. Even so, he was always devoted— some said enslaved—to his wife, Caroline of Anspach. She, a blonde, buxom woman, was his superior in talents, intelligence and common sense, whose physical attractions continued all her life to keep his interest (though they were supplemented, with her own approval, by many others), while her ability to convince him that her opinions and ideas were his own gave her the mastery of their marriage.

The Prince's first English mistress was Henrietta Howard, a young married woman who had, reputedly, sold her luxuriant hair to a wig-maker to pay her and her husband's passage to Germany to join their fellow-countrymen's dash to the Hanoverian Court in the last months of Queen Anne's life. The Howards had married for love, but Charles Howard proved a "wrong-headed, ill-tempered, obstinate, drunken and extravagant" husband.[4] Nevertheless, there is no evidence that Henrietta cuckolded him before she became the Prince's mistress in about 1710.

From his arrival in England, the younger George had shown interest in his father's new female subjects, paying court in his own abstracted way to one of his wife's maids-of-honour, Mary Bellenden. She would have none of him, dull and stolid as he was, and finally made him understand as much by tipping over the pile of coins he continually counted and recounted, and sweeping out of the royal presence.

Henrietta Howard was not so averse from George's attentions. She was a good deal older than Mary Bellenden (she was born in about 1688 and therefore was in her early twenties when she achieved her ambition) and had little of the girl's beauty; however,

> Her figure was above the middle size and well-shaped [wrote a contemporary, Lord Chesterfield]. Her face was not beautiful but pleasing. Her hair was extremely fair and remarkably fine. Her arms were square and lean, that is, ugly. Her countenance was an undecided one, and announced neither good nor ill nature, neither sense nor the want of it, neither vivacity nor dullness.[5]

Lord Hervey wrote of Henrietta Howard's character:

> Good sense, good breeding and good nature were qualities which even her enemies could not deny her; nor do I know any one good or agreeable quality which those who knew her more intimately would not as readily allow her. She was civil to everybody, friendly to many and unjust to none: in short, she had a good head and a good heart, but had to do with a man who was incapable of testing the one or valuing the other.[6]

Relations between Princess Caroline and Mrs Howard (who was one of her ladies-in-waiting) were never easy, but the wife tolerated the mistress and was glad that she was no more troublesome than she was. Less restrained was Caroline's confidante, Mrs Clayton: "They hated one another very civilly and very heartily," wrote Hervey, "for whilst Mrs Clayton was every moment like Mount Etna, ready to burst into flame, Mrs. Howard was as much mistress of her passions as of her limbs and could as easily prevent the one from showing she had a mind to strike as she could the other from giving the blow."[7]

In fact, when Charles Howard started to make trouble for his wife, pursuing her at Court and threatening to carry her off, Caroline championed Henrietta, keeping her safe within the Palace, even taking her out for an airing in her own carriage and chasing off the drink-emboldened husband when he approached them. In 1731, Howard succeeded to the earldom of Suffolk, and, since the couple had never formally divorced, his wife's new rank warranted her advancement to the office of Groom of the Stole to Caroline (a post held by Sarah Churchill under Queen Anne). By then George had been king for some four years, and Henrietta's long-endured financial hardship had been alleviated by his generosity.

However, in 1734 the Court observed that King George II had

lost all interest in the Countess: they now rarely met, and that only in public.

Sir [wrote Henrietta to George],
   As I formerly received Your Majesty's commands to acquaint you with whatever steps I should take in any of my own affairs, though it is your behaviour, sir, to me that has made me take the resolution of leaving Your Majesty's family, yet I think no consideration can dispense with my obeying these orders; this makes me take the liberty of telling Your Majesty that I shall wait upon the Queen tomorrow morning to receive any commands she may have for me before I leave her service.[8]

Such a situation delighted the gossips. They could, they said, visualise the Countess of Suffolk presenting herself to Caroline and informing her that, since the King no longer required her services, she would be withdrawing them from the Queen also. In the event, Caroline treated her kindly, and Henrietta Howard went with dignity into retirement, to marry again within a few months.

George II did not, thereafter, devote himself to his wife. He had innumerable *affaires,* mostly short and not involving the royal heart, with innumerable young women, some sent to him, so it was said, by Queen Caroline, who knew that he would always return to her, and to whom, in fact, he was frank and unrepentant about his physical needs. With Lady Deloraine, a promiscuous wanton who was his daughters' governess, George kept up a longer liaison—though again, he showed no sign of emotional involvement. She was as eager for power and influence as the Countess of Suffolk had been negligent of it: "If she got the ear of anyone in power," wrote Lord Hervey, "it might be of very bad consequence, but since 'tis only the King, I think it is of no great consequence."[9]

Hervey underestimated George II. He was not a great monarch, nor a particularly wise one, but he was sufficiently sensible to follow his wife's advice in taking Robert Walpole as his Prime Minister and letting the two of them frame most of his policies. Caroline was the only woman who ever had any real influence over the King, and she used it as discreetly as shrewdly.

At the Queen's death in 1737, George's grief proved his sincere love for her. When Caroline, dying, begged her husband to

remarry, he could only sob out an inimitable tribute to her:
"No, I shall have mistresses."

There were, indeed, many more women in George II's life
in the twenty-odd years which remained to him. Lady Deloraine's day was over (she stank of Spanish wine, George complained), but she served as a stop-gap until his Hanoverian
mistress of some years standing could be brought over to comfort
him. This was Amelia von Walmoden, a niece of the younger
Madame von Platen (just to complete the family pattern), and
she was to stay with the King until his death, taking over the
lucrative Court patronage which the Queen had wielded and
becoming Countess of Yarmouth.

There were two strong traits in the Hanoverian dynasty:
their sexual appetite and the recurring antipathy between father
and son. For years George I had been at loggerheads with his
heir: at one point, the old King even took George and Caroline's
younger children out of their custody as the most effective way
of hurting his son and daughter-in-law. Their eldest son, Frederick Lewis, had been left in Hanover when the Germans
migrated to England, and he, his grandfather's favourite, was
not called to the new Court until 1728. At first he was
welcomed by his parents but, as his typical Hanoverian proclivities began to make themselves apparent, no abuse was too bad
for Caroline to hurl at her son. Lord Hervey, her confidant,
gleefully recorded every one of the Queen's spiteful jibes against
the Prince and doubtlessly imparted them to avid listeners in
the royal household, who early on began to take sides.

Hervey did the Prince great harm at this time, reporting every
misdeed to his mother, rejecting the friendship which the two
young men had enjoyed in the first months of Frederick's life
in England. The breach between them was exacerbated by
Hervey's discovery that they shared the same mistress.

This was Anne Vane, one of Caroline's maids-of-honour, a
pretty, vapid miss who juggled her lovers without much skill.
Hervey had been the first of the two to come to her bed, and
for some time after she had won the Prince's attention, Anne
did not cast him off. But the thought that one or the other
would discover the coincidence worried Anne, and she did her
best to turn Frederick against Hervey lest their mutual confi-
dences should reveal her duplicity. When she became pregnant,
the Prince knew no better than to claim her child as his, and

set her up in style in Soho Square, where she bore a son, Corn-well Fitzfrederick. Soon, of course, the disgruntled Hervey—who now knew all—had regained his place with the foolish Anne, most likely secretly enjoying the knowledge that he was cuckolding the Prince in the bed which Frederick himself had provided. But he overplayed his hand when he attempted to blackmail her, threatening to tell Frederick of her infidelity unless she worked on the Prince to have him, Hervey, replanted in royal favour.

Anne panicked. She confessed everything to the Prince of Wales. She survived the subsequent uproar, but Hervey, inevitably, sank even lower in Frederick's estimation.

By the year 1735, however, he was tiring of 'Vanella', as Anne was named by the scurrilous versifiers who chronicled her career. Preparing for marriage with an unexceptionable German princess, the Prince followed the time-honoured convention of paying off an unwanted mistress, and was probably amazed at her haggling over the terms of the settlement which he proposed to make. In the end, of course, Frederick's will prevailed, and Anne retired to Bath, where she and her child died soon after.

Lady Archibald Hamilton (a middle-aged mother of ten children) and Grace, Countess of Middlesex, were said to be the Prince's mistresses after his marriage to Augusta of Saxe-Gotha, but so discreet were these liaisons that many believed them to be merely his friends, perhaps mother-substitutes. Certainly Frederick's married life, apart from the bitter feud which continued between him and his parents which was worsened by his new independence, was happy and peaceful.

Frederick Lewis, Prince of Wales, had prepared himself for the crown by dabbling in opposition politics, but in the event he predeceased his father, dying in 1751. Until then, his wife had been a docile, silent creature, falling in with all the Prince's schemes and backing him in his feud with his father. But as a widow, Augusta emerged as a forceful personality, as the mother of the royal heir, Frederick's son George, and as yet another butt for George II's annoyance. The new Prince of Wales, in his early teens, fully appreciated his mother's exertions on his behalf and took to his heart the man who represented her interests, the Earl of Bute. George firmly rebuffed all attempts to turn him against the Princess and would never believe the scandalmongers who coupled her name with Bute's.

Perhaps we should not believe them either, for there is no firm evidence for or against their liaison—only probability.

This innocent-minded young man, who became King George III at the age of twenty-two in 1769, was the only exception to the usually dominant characteristics of the Hanoverian kings. He had remained on good terms with his father (who admittedly died when he was only a child), and he is not known ever to have taken a mistress. Just after he came to the throne, he did profess love for one Lady Sarah Lennox (great-granddaughter of Charles II by Louise de Keroualle), but honourable proposals of marriage went with his shy approaches. Inevitably, however, the King was not allowed to mate for love but must needs take yet another German as his bride. Thereafter he lived in respectable domesticity with his Charlotte of Mecklenburg-Strelitz, and all his inherited sexual appetites went into fathering fifteen children.

It would have been a dull world for the scandalmongers of the early years of George III's reign had the cadets of the family emulated the King's virtues. They did not: who would expect that they could?

There was George's uncle William, Duke of Cumberland, the notorious 'Butcher' responsible for the massacrous aftermath of the Battle of Culloden of 1745: his tastes ran mainly to *complaisant* actresses, but there was the unsavoury episode of the unwilling little 'Savoyard' who was brought to Windsor for his delectation and then sent away on foot when she refused his advances. And there was the King's brother Henry Frederick, also Duke of Cumberland, who, after a colourful career as a rake, in 1772 announced his marriage to his mistress, a young widow named Anne Horton, without the politeness of asking the King's permission. Another brother, William Henry, Duke of Gloucester, made a duchess of the widowed Maria, Lady Waldegrave, the bastard daughter of one of the Walpoles and a little milliner. The Royal Marriage Act of 1772, compelling members of the royal family to marry only with royal approval, was framed very soon after these disturbing incidents.

But the most notorious of their generation was Princess Caroline Matilda, wife of King Christian VII of Denmark. Admittedly, her marriage was the worst possible failure, with the girl of fifteen confided to the care of a debauched and syphilitic semi-moron, whose mind would soon crumble into vacuity. It was, in fact, King Christian's doctor who took on the task of consoling the Queen : he, Johann Struensee, had political ambitions which, through Caroline Matilda, he was able to satisfy in leading the Danish government, at first with the approval of the King. However, Struensee's policies directly hit at the erstwhile-ruling Danish nobility and, in 1772, his enemies struck. Probably with the complicity of Christian VII Struensee was arrested and soon afterwards executed; Queen Caroline Matilda was put into the fortress prison of Kronborg. And there she might have remained had not George III sent a fleet into Danish waters to carry his sister into safety in his German territories. Three years later, she died, aged twenty-four.

No royal mistress in England in the eighteenth century could compare in beauty, wealth and power with those of France. Louis XV was the most fortunate of his house in possessing the glories of Madame de Pompadour in his youth and Madame du Barry in his old age. Their glamour still shines out of their portraits, those angelic faces, those shapely figures, with tiny waists encircled by flounced and frilled skirts and white breasts glimpsed through cascades of lace. But neither of these great ladies was merely a beautiful toy : the Marquise de Pompadour (whose charming title allows one to forget the name with which she was born—Jeanne Poisson, Jane Fish) had the power to make and unmake royal ministers and generals; she received ambassadors as if she had been queen in her own right; policies which she made were put into effect by royal government. Madame du Barry, who succeeded to her position after la Pompadour's death, was like a candle-flame compared with the star-burst of her predecessor : she, who had once been a bourgeoise dressmaker, had no such flair in government but made her mark with her rapacity in the sale of Court and civil service appointments. So enamoured of her was the King that, when Madame was insulted by the heedless young Dauphine Marie Antoinette (wife of Louis's heir), all Versailles trembled at the fear of his wrath, and even the girl's mother, the stalwart and pious Empress Maria Theresa, advised Marie Antoinette to make her peace with the royal mistress for the sake of the Franco-Austrian alliance.

Versailles under Louis XV was no less brilliant, and no less hedonistic, than it had been in the days of Louis XIV, typifying the grandeur and the vice of the *ancien régime*. But Louis

XV had the foresight to prophesy the storm which would engulf the aristocracy and their way of life soon after his death, in the shape of the French Revolution.

Many historians have given many different reasons for the fact that England suffered no such deluge as France at the end of the eighteenth century. Some have acknowledged the different circumstances of the two nations which had developed in different ways in the previous two centuries, some the different tempers of the two peoples: most have recognised that the English King and Queen, George and Charlotte, were far more worthy of their subjects' respect and loyalty (for all George's political ineptitude) than the foolish, ill-fated Louis XVI and Marie Antoinette.

The eighteenth century in England has been called 'the wickedest age': certainly the cartoons of Hogarth reveal the depths to which English men and women could sink in fashionable salons as well as slum tenements. But as well as being the age of the brothel and the gin-palace, it was the age of John Wesley, founder of Methodism which revitalised the religious life of the nation, and of the ordered, serene world of Jane Austen. There was a growing feeling, among the middle classes at least, that the nation's moral values were in need of thorough reformation.

George III's granddaughter, Queen Victoria, has been hailed as the agent by which the monarchy became respectable after years of disrepute, but George III himself, and his staid Queen Charlotte, with their domestic bliss and their circle of quiet, middle-class intimates, had done their share first to elevate the monarchy.

It was scarcely their fault that their sons undid their good word. The Hanoverian blood flowed strong and wild in the veins of the future King George IV and his brother the Duke of York, so strongly as to counteract their parents' moral teaching. Their careers are a fine argument in favour of heredity over environment as the moulder of character. . . .

11

Princess Fitz

The Royal Marriage Act which entered the statute books in 1772 was a curious piece of legislation, proceeding directly from King George III's fear that his dynasty would be defamed and defiled by the mingling of royal and common blood. The marriages of his brothers the Dukes of Cumberland and Gloucester had alerted the King to this danger: it was too late to prevent their offences, but, with this Act, he intended to forestall similar *mésalliances* by his own children.

The Act ordained that any marriage made by a member of the royal family would be valid only if the King's permission had first been obtained. The only way of circumventing this edict was for a prince or princess bent on a union forbidden by the King to be over twenty-five years of age, to give the Privy Council six months' notice of their intent: Parliament was to have the right to censure the match but not to prevent it forcibly.

In fact, the Royal Marriage Act did not prevent two of the King's sons from secretly marrying commoners,* and, incongruously, it would allow one of those princes, the future King George IV, to make a second marriage which, for any other man, would have been bigamous but which, for him under the terms of the Act, was perfectly legal. George, then Prince of Wales, married one Maria Fitzherbert in a secret ceremony in December 1785. Certainly, his father would never have given his consent to that match, for not only was Maria a commoner but she was also a Catholic. Under the Act of Settlement of 1701, any member of the royal family marrying a Catholic automatically forfeited his right to inherit the crown.† How-

* See page 161 for the marriage of Prince Augustus.
† The ban is still in force today. A member of the royal family may marry a Protestant dissenter, a Buddhist, a Mohammedan or an atheist—providing the monarch or Parliament consents, and retain a place in the succession to the throne: but by marrying a Catholic, he or she forfeits that right.

ever, since George's marriage was not publicised, he was not prosecuted under the terms of either of the Acts relating to royal marriages. And, since the Royal Marriage Act could release him from that first marriage, when he wished to make a more regular union with a princess, he was able to do so, even though his first wife was still living. George had the flexible type of conscience which could accommodate such chicanery.

King George III and Queen Charlotte had recognised and faced up to the hereditary vices of the Hanoverian dynasty, but they thought they had prepared their children for a life of virtue by educating them themselves, laying a firm moral basis for their future careers. They were to be bitterly disappointed.

The eldest prince, George, was only sixteen years old when, in 1779, he fell in love with one of his sisters' governesses, Mary Hamilton, six years his senior. For several months they corresponded, secretly, under the pseudonyms of 'Palemon' and 'Miranda'. But Mary Hamilton was not the initiator of this innocent into the delights of sexuality: she was, she declared, as a sister to him and would exercise this freedom to tell him his faults: George took this in good part and submitted to her mature judgment his adolescent views on life, his plans for his future and the patterns for his new clothes. When, about a year later, the Prince fell in love with another woman, he poured out his heart to Mary, assuring her that he would always treasure her friendship, though he did not heed her warning against the siren who now enthralled him.

The new love was a twenty-one-year-old actress, already a rising star in the firmament of the London theatre: Mary Robinson. She was his 'Perdita', he her 'Florizel', from the characters in Shakespeare's *Winter's Tale* in which she had had such success.

Contemporary cartoonists, alerted to the situation by widespread gossip and rumour, were soon turning out sketches of the lovers in idyllic settings. However, before their works were out of print, they were out of date: 'Perdita' was discarded for the charms of one Mrs Grace Dalrymple Elliott, a bourgeoise divorcée. (The satirists need not have feared: over the next half-century, they would recoup their losses over the Robinson engravings, and make a mint of money, with their cartoons of George's amorous escapades and those of his younger brothers.)

Now Mary Hamilton's warnings might have struck home,

for Mrs Robinson let it be known that she possessed many fervent love-letters from the Prince, from which she might, for a consideration, part. 'Perdita' would not admit that she was blackmailing George: she took his handsome settlement (in exchange for the letters) only to restore his "peace of mind", she said. In fact, some fifteen years later, she reappeared, now partly paralysed and prematurely aged, to make further demands on his purse, and the Prince, good-naturedly, forgot the bitter past and was a regular visitor to her couch until her death, at the age of forty, in 1800.

By that date, George was a middle-aged *roué* with many mistresses to the credit of his reputation and the debit of his exchequer. There was Madame von Hardenburg, wife of a Hanoverian diplomat, who threatened a scandal unless the Prince restored her to him; Lady Melbourne, mother of the future Prime Minister; Georgiana, Duchess of Devonshire, the great political hostess, and numerous ladies of lesser fame, actresses and singers, matrons and maids, courtiers and courtesans, who saw the Prince comfortably through the early 1780s.

Then, fatefully, George met and fell in love with Maria Fitzherbert. Like most of the women who attracted him, she was several years his senior (she was born in 1756, he in 1762); unlike the rest, she had some pretension to virtue.

Maria Fitzherbert, née Smythe, was the daughter of a gentleman-soldier, and had been twice widowed by the time she met the Prince, in 1784. She was handsome and rich, acceptable as his companion in society, but she was a Catholic and took her religion seriously: she would not, she firmly announced, enjoy sinful intimacy with her future sovereign.

George was mad with love. He even attempted suicide, or gave a creditable performance of doing so, to scare Maria into acquiescence. He wrung from her a promise to marry him, but immediately afterwards, she took fright and hastily left the country.

Forbidden by the King to follow her, the Prince despatched letter after letter begging Mrs Fitzherbert to return. He could not live without her, he claimed: "Save me, save me, save me, on my knees I conjure you, from myself"[1] After a year of such pleas and of tidings of the Prince's misery, Maria relented and came home. Within the month she had married him.

Without the interference of the Royal Marriage Act, the

wedding would certainly have been legal. Admittedly, the clergyman (an Anglican, despite Maria's scruples) was not of any great repute, being recently released from a debtors' prison, but Maria's uncle and brothers attended as witnesses and everything needful to make the union sacred in the sight of God was provided. But the Royal Marriage Act, and the Act of Settlement, could not be ignored, and while George loved Maria, he could not offer her the place properly belonging to his wife. Maria herself felt conscience-clear in cohabiting with the Prince now: the fact that she was thought to be only his mistress worried her not at all.

Inevitably, there were rumours that the couple were married, but when questions were asked in Parliament about the Prince's marital status, one of his friends rose to deny that George had married Maria, relying on George's own word to him. Mrs Fitzherbert was called by his circle of intimates 'Princess Fitz', but very few guessed that she was indeed his wife by canon law if not by constitutional law. George's brothers and sisters accepted her at the royal table; she ruled his household and received his friends; it was she who introduced the Prince to the delights of Brighthelmstone, the small seaside resort on the south coast which, as Brighton, is now still best known for its association with illicit liaisons.

King George and Queen Charlotte had not the pleasure of 'Princess Fitz's' acquaintance. They lived largely in retirement, their personal friends drawn from their attendants and a narrow coterie of middle-class, staid, sober and respectable citizens. In contrast, Prince George was at the centre of a rowdy, extravagant crowd, whose social cavortings and political opposition to the government caused the King much sorrow. Relations between royal father and son never deteriorated as far as those of previous generations, but their political estrangement was just one more pressure on the over-burdened George III.

The King suffered from a rare blood disease (transmitted, it is said, from his Stuart ancestors), which contemporary medicine could not diagnose. The treatment which he received only exacerbated his condition and, in the autumn of 1788, it was feared that he would die. But George III survived, and his heir, bitterly disappointed at having his succession to the throne postponed further, was left to continue his racketing, denied any share in his father's rule.

The Prince of Wales was not faithful to his wife. He hurt her cruelly by his meanderings. For some years she bore with his continual infidelities, for they seemed always temporary infatuations, not a serious threat to her own position; but George's liaison with Frances Villiers, Countess of Jersey, went deeper than the rest, and at last Maria would stand no more. In 1794 the couple parted.

However, there was a more serious and potent pressure on the Prince to cast off his wife than the claims of a new mistress: he decided that it was time to do his duty to the crown and marry a suitable princess. In years gone by, even before he met Mrs Fitzherbert, the Prince had let it be known that he would never accept one of the dull, ugly 'German fraus' such as his forefathers had taken to wife: he would leave his brother Frederick as his heir, he had declared. Now, he resolved to marry—largely with an eye to an increased grant from Parliament which would help him clear his debts and live in greater style: the building of his sumptuous Pavilion at Brighton was impoverishing him.

The fact that George was married already troubled him not at all. Indeed, he was encouraged to presume himself legally a bachelor by the judgment which a Court of Privileges made against the marriage of his brother Augustus, that very summer of 1794, declaring that since the Prince and Lady Augusta Murray had married in contravention of the Royal Marriage Act, their union was null and void. As George reasoned, his own marriage with Maria Fitzherbert would be invalid on the same terms, so that he was free to look for another bride.

The Prince of Wales could blame no one but himself for the error of his choice. He himself selected his paternal cousin Caroline of Brunswick-Wolfenbuttel from the available princesses of Europe, though it is possible that he had not heard the rumours about her which even his own mother did not care to confide to him. On paper, Caroline seemed an ideal candidate for the royal bed and crown: a princess, a German, young and supposedly unspoiled by contact with the great world. In fact, the girl was devoid of royal bearing, vulgar in language and habits (the British envoy sent to bring her to George had to speak severely to his charge to make her wash her person and her underwear); her greatest friend at home was her father's mistress. Caroline was no dewy-eyed innocent to be shocked by

Ehrengard Melusina von der Schulenberg, one of the Hanoverian mistresses brought to England by King George I in 1714.

Henrietta Howard, Countess of Suffolk, the chief English mistress of George II—and Mistress of the Robes to his wife, Queen Caroline.

'Baise moi'—a cartoonist's view of George IV with his last mistress, the Marchioness of Conyngham, in 1820.

Mary Anne Clarke at the Bar of the House of Commons, enjoying the furore created by her revelations of scandals discrediting her former lover, Frederick, Duke of York.

her husband's deficiencies but a forthright, strong-willed, though ill-judging young woman, with no sense of her royal vocation and none of that patient fortitude which allowed many other princesses to keep their dignity when faced with unhappy marriages.

When Princess Caroline arrived in England in April 1795, the leader of her reception-committee was Lady Jersey, still mistress of the Prince of Wales and determined not to be ousted by his bride. All the charm which Caroline possessed lay in her youth and freshness, and this the older woman speedily destroyed by dressing her in a formal Court gown and painting her face thickly with cosmetics. The Prince took one look at his future wife and turned pale, demanding brandy to fortify him.

The bottle was also to the fore on the wedding-day, 8 April 1795. The Prince was so drunk that he spent his wedding-night in a stupor on the bedroom floor, his head in the grate. Nevertheless, almost exactly nine months later, on 7 January 1796, an offspring of this unhappy union appeared: a daughter, who was named Charlotte for her paternal grandmother.

In the first months of their marriage, the Prince and Princess of Wales had made an attempt to accommodate themselves to each other, but with little success. Caroline could behave herself in the kindly but formal presence of her parents-in-law, but when alone with her husband or entertaining his friends, she threw off all restraint and appeared noisy, coarse, impertinent and wayward. And she was publicly rude to Lady Jersey, who, with years of Court training behind her, could snub the Princess effectively while maintaining the appearance of graceful politeness. But worst of all, in the eyes of the Prince, Caroline was acquiring a following of sympathisers and champions, who pitied her plight as neglected wife (the Prince spent as little time as possible in her company, it was noticed) and reviling her husband, even in the columns of the national Press. George's political excursions had long been censured by those who condemned his alignment with Opposition politicians, and his marital problems added fuel to the flames which his political enemies were always stoking.

For some months before the birth of their child, the Prince and Princess seem to have been contemplating a form of separation and, while rumours of the breach spread, the spring of 1796 found the couple exchanging long screeds of accusations and excuses, demands and concessions, which were intended to clear the way for their parting. At first, Caroline conceded that she would continue to live in the same house with her husband, as long as Lady Jersey was dismissed and providing always that, should the child Charlotte die, George would never demand of her another heir to the throne. That April, the Prince wrote what he intended to be the last of the series of letters which had passed between himself and his wife:

> Nature has not made us suitable to each other. Tranquil and comfortable society is, however, in our power; let our intercourse be restricted to that, and I will distinctly subscribe to the condition which you required . . . that even in the event of any accident happening to my daughter, which I trust Providence in its mercy will avert, I shall not infringe the terms of the restriction by purposing, at any period, a connection of a more particular nature. I shall now finally close this disagreeable correspondence, trusting that as we have completely explained ourselves to each other, the rest of our lives will be passed in uninterrupted tranquillity.[2]

Had Caroline now been discreet, she might have won her husband's respect at last. She was not: she protested to the King against George's ill-treatment of her, and against the humiliation of having Lady Jersey still among her attendants, all the while currying favour with the populace, taking the role of ill-used, tragic heroine allotted to her by political propagandists. The Prince became so unpopular that he was booed in the streets, and many feared that violent revolution (such as France had suffered only a few years earlier) would follow on his accession to the throne should his father die in the near future.

The King was inclined to blame his son for the scandal to which his marriage was giving rise. The Prince could, said George III, have moulded Caroline to better character and docility if he had exerted himself to overcome her natural faults. Nor would he countenance the formal separation which both parties were now demanding. "You seem to look on your union with the Princess as merely of a private nature," the King wrote to his son at the end of May, "and totally put out of sight that as Heir Apparent of the Crown your marriage is a public act, wherein the kingdom is concerned; that therefore a separation cannot be brought forward by the mere interference of relations."[3]

Nevertheless, a separation there must be. Finally, the Prince won his father's approval to Caroline's moving out of Carlton House, his London residence—though she was to keep apartments there to be used when royal ceremonies demanded her presence at his side, and permitted her to set up house in the village of Charlton, on the Thames. This arrangement satisfied all parties—for the time being.

The months of waiting for the birth of his child had imposed a heavy strain on George, always fearful that the baby would be born dead, or die soon after birth, and that he would have to resume relations with his wife to fulfil his obligations to the crown. When the Princess Charlotte appeared, strong and healthy, the Prince had a minor nervous collapse, fancying himself near to death and feverishly preparing himself for Divine reckoning. It was at this point that he penned his Will, naming his "beloved and adored Maria Fitzherbert" as the main beneficiary of his extensive property, and ending the document thus:

> To thee, therefore, my Maria, my wife, my life, my soul, do I bid my last adieu; round thee shall my soul forever hover as thy guardian angel, for as I never ceased to adore thee whilst living, so shall I ever be watchful over thee and protect thee against every evil. Farewell, dearest angel . . . think of thy DEPARTED HUSBAND, shed a tear o'er his memory and his grave and then recollect that no woman ever yet was so loved or adored by man as you were and are by him.[4]

But if George had convinced himself that he had never ceased to love Mrs Fitzherbert, she, when approached by the Prince with a view to her returning to him, was not so easily persuaded. It took George more than four years to free himself from Lady Jersey and overcome Maria's scruples, and before she did return to him, in the spring of 1800, she had taken care to apply to the Vatican to have papal confirmation that her relations with the Prince were acceptable to the Church: the Pope assured her that, in the eyes of God and Catholics, she was the indubitable, only, legal wife of the Prince of Wales.

Under Maria's care, George lived a more regular life, drinking and eating less (though he was still enormously fat), and taking more exercise, but 'the Prince of Pleasure' spent as prodigally as ever, his debts mounting to ruinous proportions to keep up his luxurious living-standards. Britain was at war with France (and had been for several years), but at Carlton House and the Brighton Pavilion there was no sign of tightening the belt for the war effort. Forbidden any real part in the nation's exertions against Napoleon, George merely played at soldiering, more conversant with the etiquette of military honour and with the details of regimental colours than with strategy and tactics. He drilled his men on Brighton Beach, looking wistfully, so it was said, across the Channel towards the enemy whom he never saw.

Mrs Fitzherbert was supremely content in her life with the Prince. They were childless but, to her delight, she had been awarded the custody of a small girl, Minnie Seymour, daughter of an old friend who had recently died. Unfortunately for Maria's peace of mind, the negotiations with the Seymour family for Minnie had thrown George together with the child's aunt, the Marchioness of Hertford, with dire consequences for his 'marriage'.

Isabella Seymour, Lady Hertford, was another of the amply-proportioned grandmothers who so often attracted the Prince, and she had some idea of propriety even if not of morality. Her delicacy forbade her, she averred, from receiving or being received by the Prince of Wales in private: Mrs Fitzherbert was summoned to chaperone the portly love-birds and forced to listen to their cooing. As in the first phase of their liaison, Maria had learned to bear with George's minor lapses of virtue, but now she was again placed in a quite intolerable position. Not all the Prince's protestations of continuing love could compensate her for the humiliations dealt out by Lady Hertford. With a fine show of amity, the couple parted in 1809—this time for ever.

But where, all this while, was the real Princess of Wales, Caroline? She had certainly not been inconspicuous in the years since she had given up the pretence of being the Prince's wife. As the new century opened, there were ever-increasing rumours as to 'goings-on' at her Blackheath home (to which she had moved from Charlton in 1798): it was even said that a small boy whom she was bringing up, known as William Austin, was her son. Caroline had reputedly asserted that, rather than give him up, she would declare that his father was the Prince himself. Until then, George III had been sympathetic to his daughter-in-law; now he demanded an enquiry into her conduct. The 'Delicate Investigation', as it was called, was launched in the summer of 1806, with an examination of the Princess's staff and friends. It was proved that William Austin was in fact a charity case taken in by Caroline, but her own conduct was open, it was said, "to very unfavourable interpretations". She had taken lovers, that much was certain, most of them naval officers stationed at nearby Greenwich.

However, the reprimand and warning which the Princess of Wales received from the King did not much dampen her spirits.

In 1811, George III's illness, and the barbarous treatment which it had received from his physicians, had so far worsened for him to be pronounced mad and consigned to the care of medical guardians. At last his son came to power, as Regent, though under strict limitations which infuriated him. Britain was still at war with the French Emperor Napoleon and his allies: there were continual invasion-scares, and the political situation was eminently unstable. Nevertheless, for all George's inexperience in government, and despite the heavy odds against Britain's withstanding the combined might of France and her satellites, the nation, and its new ruler, survived the testing years. In 1814 Europe was offered peace at last.

The end of the war opened up the Continent to British travellers after years of confinement. One of the most eager to embark on the Grand Tour was Princess Caroline who, in August 1814, shrugged off the restraints of her adoptive country and began to career round Europe noisily and hilariously, leaving a train of lovers in her wake and carrying one of them, the Italian Bartolomeo Pergami with her, as *cicerone*, *cicisbeo* and *gigolo* (Italian epiphets which have passed into common usage largely by the willingness of English lady-tourists to pay for Italian love).

No one missed Caroline, except perhaps her daughter Charlotte, now in her teens. Very early on, the young Princess had been taken out of her mother's care and cloistered with her elderly maiden aunts at Windsor, and the Princess of Wales had been allowed only occasional visits from her daughter for fear of what Caroline might say to her. Such fears were justified: Caroline's influence over the girl was obviously harmful, encouraging as she did Charlotte's aversion from her father and his family by presenting herself as the victim of George's cruelty. The Princess had even, wilfully, mischievously, tried to ruin her daughter's reputation, locking Charlotte alone in a bedroom with a man reputed to be her own lover. Fortunately, this Captain Hesse (said to be the son of George's brother the Duke of York) had some vestiges of decency, and the young Princess emerged unharmed—no thanks to her mother.

In 1816 Charlotte was married off to Prince Leopold of Saxe-Coburg-Saalfeld, a penniless German princeling only too glad to take on and attempt to tame his turbulent young bride in exchange for a generous income and the prospect of a consort's crown. But seventeen months after her wedding, the Princess died in childbirth.

Despite the fact that the Prince Regent and his surviving brothers and sisters were twelve in number, not one of them could muster a legitimate child who might be heir to the throne in the next generation. As matters now stood, the crown would pass from one elderly prince to another, then to the princesses, then to their paternal cousins, over in Brunswick: surely a hazardous situation for the already shaky British monarchy.

There was no suggestion that the Prince should recall his erring wife and attempt to produce a new heir to the throne of her body, to replace Charlotte. On the other hand, it was feasible that he might divorce Caroline and remarry. To this end the government empowered three eminent men to undertake investigations into Caroline's conduct: they established themselves at Milan (not far from her love-nest, the Villa d'Este on Lake Como) in the summer of 1818. On their return to England, that autumn, the commissioners carried with them ample evidence of Caroline's intimacy with Pergami, collected from the depositions of servants: the Italian had been seen to fondle her naked breasts in public, to caress her thigh; they had slept, during a coach-journey, with their arms around each other; Pergami had been seen many times in her bedroom, with and without his clothes; he had been alone with the Princess while she was in her bath: all this backstairs gossip was seriously written down and preserved for use at a future date.

It had initially been hoped that the evidence against Caroline could be used to force her to renounce her rights or even to procure George's divorce from her before King George III should die, making her George IV's queen. Unfortunately for his peace of mind, however, George succeeded his father, on 29 January 1820, before any decision had been made.

Caroline was still in Italy at that time, and, refusing to accept the £50,000 a year offered for her agreement not to return to Britain, she made her way slowly but relentlessly northward, landing at Dover on 5 June. Exactly a month later, a Bill of Pains and Penalties was read out in the House of Lords, denouncing Caroline's adultery with Pergami and demanding her divorce from George.

'The capital in turmoil' is an old cliché applied to many historical situations: but it is valid for the summer of 1820, when mobs crowded the London streets clamouring for Caroline to appear, gawping at displays of lit and enlarged colour-frames in her honour in which some of the most popular set-pieces depicted Caroline as "the angel of innocence" and her detractors as "an Italian female wretch" in the pay of the Pope and "a Turkish bribed accuser of Royal innocence"; even the soldiery stationed in London were suspected of sympathy with Caroline, to the extent that, when they refused to give up their ammunition when they came off duty, they were hustled out of the city lest they turn against the King. Caricaturists 'cashed in' on the situation, running off thousands of sheets of scurrilous cartoons against George IV, and some, admittedly, against Caroline, for the minority who reviled her. As the day of the Queen's 'trial' approached, hundreds of agitators, mainly Radical in their politics, poured into the capital, many of them drunk and violent, most of them ready to threaten the carriages of any royal minister who dared appear on the streets.

The hearing of the case in the House of Lords opened on 17 August and continued for eleven weeks. Evidence was brought by the prosecution to show the adulterous relationship between Caroline and Pergami. Sordid and prurient in content, it was often muddled and imprecise as to date and place, and the Italian and British witnesses were frequently discreditable in the eyes of the assembled peers. Pergami was not present—he had been left safely in Italy; but Caroline attended many of the sessions, though she was not permitted to speak in her own defence: King George, of course, remained at Windsor, comforted by the protective embrace of his latest mistress, Lady Conyngham.

In the past, circumstantial evidence has often damned innocent and guilty alike in British courts of justice, but in the case of Queen Caroline it was not sufficient to find her guilty. As the government majority dwindled with the third reading of the Bill in the Lords, the King's ministers hesitated to take it into the Commons, where it would almost certainly have been rejected. Sooner than risk the government's falling over this issue, Prime Minister Liverpool withdrew the Bill of Pains and Penalties, and Parliament was prorogued.

London, and several other cities, celebrated Caroline's victory with bonfires and bells. The Queen was rapturously greeted whenever she left her house, and her champions—such as Alderman Wood and Henry Brougham, who had managed her propaganda and marshalled her defence in the Lords—were hailed as national heroes. The King sulked, railing at his ministers who had, he considered, bungled the affair and threatening to replace them with their Whig adversaries.

George's coronation had already been postponed from August 1820, but it could wait no longer. 19 July 1821 was the date now set. With or without tongue in cheek, that May Caroline applied to the Prime Minister for information as to the arrangements made to accommodate her in Westminster Abbey on coronation day, and cannot have been surprised when she was denied any role in the ceremony. Nevertheless, soon after the service began, she arrived at the Abbey, dressed in all her finery, only to be refused admittance because she had no ticket. But now there was no one to cheer her on, no one willing to force an entry for her: the fickle mob had tired of their heroine and even hissed and booed as she retired from the precincts.

On the evening of 30 July, while attending a coronation pageant at Drury Lane, the Queen complained of sharp pains in the abdomen. Her physicians diagnosed "inflammation of the bowels" and bled her and dosed her with purges. But that is no way to deal with appendicitis. Caroline was in agonies for the next week, sometimes delirious with the pain. Then, on the evening of 8 August she went into convulsions, and she died at about 10.30 p.m.

George IV did not immediately seek a bride, wed her and bed her and provide a new heir. Lady Conyngham's bulky figure continued to fill his vision and his bed for all that remained to him of his life. After all, his younger brothers had been stirred by Princess Charlotte's death to do their duty, and the King now had two nephews and a niece to carry on the royal line, so why should George hazard his comfortable life on the amiability and fertility of a stranger? And so he ended his life as his adult life had begun: in self-indulgence and hedonism.

But if all he did as a man and as a monarch draws one to conclude that George IV acted primarily and always from self-indulgence and self-love, he had once loved so strongly as to hazard, albeit temporarily, his own interests: after his death in 1830, his body was examined and it was found that he still wore a locket, enclosing Maria Fitzherbert's likeness, given to him so many years before, and which he had promised to wear all his life.

When Mrs. Fitzherbert heard that the King had been buried with the locket around his neck, she said nothing, but tears welled up in her eyes.

12

Duke or Darling

Satirists and cartoonists never lacked subjects for their art during the lifetime of George IV, with his *amours* and his marital problems, his obesity and his eccentricities, but he was not their only butt in these years: his brothers' lives also had their irregularities, too spicily amusing to be ignored then or now.

There was, for instance, the second son of George III, Frederick, Duke of York. He was the first of the princes to marry: he realised his responsibility to continue the dynasty, since his brother George was then so infatuated with his supposed mistress Mrs Fitzherbert that it seemed unlikely that he would do so himself. But Princess Frederica of Prussia, Frederick's bride of 1791, proved barren. She compensated partly for this failure, however, by making no complaint against her husband's consistent infidelities, and remained on good terms with him to the end of her life, retiring to the country to busy herself with charitable works and finding solace for his neglect of her in the company of innumerable lap-dogs.

There would have been nothing remarkable, or particularly censurable, to the majority opinion of the time, in the Duke of York's string of mistresses, for the most part nonentities who were housed discreetly in London suburbs and not flaunted in public, had not one of them distinguished herself by meddling in public affairs: her revelations would strike at the career and the prestige of her lover and for a while threaten to ruin him.

This was Mary Anne Clarke, a bricklayer's daughter from Bowl and Pin Alley in the City, who had arrived in the ducal bed—via several others—in about 1804. The allowance which Frederick settled on her, £1,000 a year with a house and servants and carriage, was generous by any standards, but Mary Anne could not resist laying aside a little nest-egg against the inevitable day when he should tire of her. This she did by taking bribes for her influence over the Duke in gaining army promotions and commissions for her protégés (as Commander-in-Chief, Frederick was the fount of such prizes, for which there was a good deal of competition). Whether, in fact, Mary Anne had as much influence as was thought became a matter of debate— in Parliament. . . .

By 1808 the Duke of York had discarded Mrs Clarke for one Mrs Cary, but Mary Anne was not disconsolate. She had swiftly been taken up by two gentlemen who were very kind to her : Major Dodd and Colonel Wardle. They did not mind how much she prattled about her reign in the ducal *ménage*, and listened attentively when she boasted of her 'perks'. Then, on 27 January 1809, Colonel Wardle laid before the House of Commons serious charges against the Duke, demanding an enquiry into his conduct with regard to the staffing of the army, using Mary Anne's revelations as the basis of his case. As might be expected, the Opposition members raised a cheer at the thought of striking against the military command which was so apparently inept in its management of the war with France.

In the public enquiry which followed, Mrs Clarke admitted nothing during her several examinations and she lied inexpertly, but the saucy answers which she offered, parrying the thrusts of the commissioners, won her a host of new admirers (one member was so overcome by her charm that he passed her a note offering three hundred guineas for the chance to have 'supper' with her). However, the evidence of other witnesses revealed her culpability—one of them was her own friend, Elizabeth Taylor, a brothel-keeper from Chelsea, who could remember, so she said, a conversation which had passed between the Duke and Mary Anne some time before, in which he threatened to "cut up" a certain officer who had slighted his mistress.

Nevertheless, nothing could be adduced to prove that the Duke of York had been influenced by Mrs Clarke in any of the promotions he had made or in his awarding of commissions. Undoubtedly he had 'made up' some of the men who had bought Mary Anne's influence, but it seemed likely that there were as many more who had risen without her help, and that some men who had bribed her had not had their money's worth. By the end of the enquiry, the extent of the Duke's involvement was still in doubt—though it seemed eminently unlikely that he could have been ignorant that Mary Anne was supplementing her income—and, with the government rallied to his defence, a majority of Members decided in his favour.

However, the proceedings had been very unpleasant for the Duke. His love-letters to his mistress had been read aloud in the House, some of them published in the newspapers. So notorious had the *affaire* become that throughout England coin-tossers no longer called "Heads or tails?" but "Duke or Darling?". (It was ironic that the royal mistress who had posed for Britannia on the coins should now be replaced by another in popular parlance.)

Despite his exoneration, Frederick found that 'mud sticks': he felt compelled to resign his command. In fact, two years later, he was re-instated: post-enquiry evidence had shown that Mary Anne Clarke was not a repentant sinner who had hazarded her own reputation to reveal corruption but an informer paid by Wardle to blacken Frederick's name.

In 1810, both Wardle and his friend Dodd were further vilified in a publication entitled *The Rival Princes*, a product of Mrs Clarke's own pen which purported to show that York's younger brother Edward, Duke of Kent, had been behind the whole affair, that it was he who had instigated Dodd (his own military secretary) and Wardle's attack on York, in the hope of his succeeding to his brother's command. She said that Kent had offered her £10,000, through Dodd, if her evidence could accomplish it. In fact, the matter of Kent's involvement in the scandal had already been raised in 1809, during the enquiry, and he had already attempted to clear his name, but now he sponsored a public reply to the charges, which included Dodd's own statement that the Duke was innocent of undermining his brother's command. York and Kent were at daggers drawn for some months, and when they were reconciled, it was only formally.

The Duke of York had learned his lesson from the Mary Anne affair. In later years he turned from unreliable bourgeoise mistresses and took the more worldly-wise Duchess of Rutland to his heart and bed. He lived on without further worries—apart from his always-troublesome debts—until 1827, three years before the death of his elder brother, whom he might have succeeded on the throne.

In 1814 Mary Anne Clarke's career in libel and slander came to an end when she was imprisoned for nine months for her attack on yet another man who had earned her enmity, the Chancellor of the Irish Exchequer. She served her term and then went into exile, reputedly unabashed and able fully to enjoy the nearly forty years of life remaining to her.

The qualification of the third royal brother, William, Duke of Clarence, to be included among the mistress-keepers of his family is surely unique. Trained for naval command from his youth, William inevitably fell a prey to the prostitutes of the ports at home and abroad: he is even said to have brought home a West Indian concubine, improbably named 'Wowski', to the horror of his superiors. But it was after he was confined to land, in his mid-twenties, that he distinguished himself: he took as mistress a comic actress, Dorothy Jordan, with whom he was to live, contentedly and devotedly, for the next twenty-odd years, and who gave him ten children.

William's liaison opened, and continued to its end, in a blaze of publicity. Mrs Jordan was, after all, as public a figure as he himself, renowned for her performances in 'breeches parts' on the London stage and in extensive tours through the provinces. She was, undoubtedly, vulgar and often foul-mouthed, even by Regency standards, but then William was no Prince Charming himself but rather of the common run of contemporary seamen, rowdy and randy, drink-sodden and none too clean. He had much in common with his erstwhile commander, Horatio Nelson, whose *affaire* with the beautiful Lady Hamilton so marred that great man's reputation.

As the years passed, ten little 'Fitzclarences' appeared to tie William to his home and (assisted by three offspring of Mrs Jordan's former passions) to strain his income to the limit. The Prince made his mistress a generous allowance, which he endeavoured to pay even when worst-pressed by his creditors, but often he was so poor that Dorothy was forced to supplement the family budget by returning to the stage, still an adept exponent of her lively art even when her youth and slight beauty had faded into wrinkles and fat. To the versifiers of the time, this absurd situation was heaven-sent; they declaimed,

> As Jordan's high and mighty squire
> Her playhouse profits deigns to skim,
> Some folks audaciously enquire
> If *he* keeps *her* or *she* keeps *him*!

It was in fact money (or rather, the want of it) which brought the idyll to an end—and idyll it was, from the evidence of the couple's ever-loving correspondence. Only by marriage, which would bring an increased grant from Parliament and, hopefully, a generous dowry, could William ever hope to clear his mountainous debts. He had his eye on an English heiress who could, by the stroke of a pen on a money-order, release him from his creditors, and who might give him yet more children, eligible, as the Fitzclarences could never be, to inherit the throne.

Unfortunately, though Mrs Jordan went uncomplainingly out of William's life, he could not immediately replace her with a bride. The heiress rejected him, and the many other ladies to whom he proposed were equally scornful of his advances. Only in 1818 was his persistence rewarded by acceptance by a suitable candidate to share his future throne: the Princess Adelaide of Saxe-Meiningen, no heiress but as orthodox a choice as anyone could desire. At twenty-six she was not a youthful belle, but she was sensible and kind, even willing to mother the wayward Fitzclarences who teemed in her household. Adelaide's own babies died and, in later years, she was nationally reviled for her supposed meddling in politics (at the time of the controversial Reform Bill), but she was just such a wife as William needed, able to control his drinking, to moderate his language and to keep him not only faithful but respectable throughout his reign, which the nation demanded after the flagrant immorality of George IV's Court.

The next royal brother, Edward, Duke of Kent, was as domestically inclined as William. He too had had youthful indiscretions; he too settled down, in his twenties, with a woman to whom he could remain faithful, and in his case, for more than a quarter of a century.

Kent had been trained in the army as his elder brother William had been in the navy. Ever since his teens he had scarcely been more than a few months at home, going from one foreign posting to another, until, after a not particularly creditable career, he settled in England in 1803. The besetting fear of army officers abroad was loneliness: to assuage his own, while on duty in Gibraltar in 1790, Edward had sent to France for an amiable French companion. The woman who arrived, supplied by his agent, was Julie St Laurent, a neat, pretty little woman whose origins have never been satisfactorily traced.

In the years that followed, she went with the Duke from one foreign garrison to another, from the heat of the Mediterranean Rock to the winter snows of Montreal. When the couple arrived in England, in 1803, Julie was deposited discreetly in a house at Ealing, where she acted as hostess to Edward's brothers and his political friends with admirable aplomb.

Unlike his two eldest brothers, Kent was neither rake nor roisterer. On duty, he was a martinet, capable of hanging mutineers and lashing defaulters without mercy; at home, he was all mildness and affection. The royal family tended to deride Edward as a hypocrite, never giving due credit to the sincerity of his good intentions: they laughed at his many charities and his church-going and sneered at his Radical cronies. The Clarke affair of 1810 only confirmed their low opinion of him, and the Prince of Wales could never look at his brother without distaste.

Unlike the Duke of Clarence, the Duke of Kent was childless. But that seems only to have bound him closer to Madame St Laurent. When, at last, he could stave off marriage no longer, he was in agonies lest his Julie should be hurt by his desertion of her after so many years of happiness.

The couple were living in Brussels at the time (in one of a series of vain attempts to retrench on expenditure), and the Duke did his best to prevent English gossip about his marriage from reaching his mistress—even to the extent of begging newspaper editors to keep his name out of their columns. But one, the editor of the *Morning Chronicle*, printed a notice of Edward's impending marriage in early February 1817, and it was reproduced in one of the Continental papers taken by Madame. The Duke described his *petite amie*'s reaction: "It produced *no* heat or violence on *her* part, but a scene more truly distressing or heart-breaking than *any* I ever yet went thro', yet the whole of which does equal honour to her head and to her heart . . . it has made a very deep impression on her, the subject is frequently reverted to, and occasions infinitely uncomfortable moments to both."[1]

Even as Edward and Julie enjoyed a last peaceful summer together, the Duke's chosen bride, the widowed Victoire, Princess of Leiningen, was debating whether to accept him. Then, in November, Edward's niece the Princess Charlotte died, and more urgency was introduced into his suit by the need to provide a new heir to the throne. That same month, the *Morning Chronicle* published his intent—Julie came upon it over break-fast: "an extraordinary noise and a strong convulsive movement in Madame St Laurent's throat"[2] alerted her lover to her distress.

By the following March all had been arranged. The Duke pretended that he was leaving his mistress for only a short visit to his family, but she knew that he would not return. She let him go without one reproach. Two months later Edward was married. Twenty months after that, in January 1820, he died.

Though the Duke of Kent had broken completely with Julie St Laurent and had to come to his cheerful, rosy German bride with good intentions to love and cherish her, he never ceased to care for his mistress of so many years. As far as his means—and his creditors—allowed, he was generous to her, and, adding a kind personal touch, begged his friends to rally round and comfort her in his absence. Julie lived on, with no new protector, in Paris; the date of her death is unknown, but it is not impossible that she may have lived to see Kent's daughter ascend the throne as Queen Victoria in 1837.

So discreet had Edward been that the general public knew nothing of his liaison with Madame St Laurent (apart from Mary Anne Clarke's spiteful hints about "his old French lady" and his "discovery of the St Lawrence" in *The Rival Princes*) until the early twentieth century, when the revelations of a con-temporary, his acquaintance Thomas Creevey, were published. Queen Victoria may have heard of her father's long liaison, but she is not known ever to have referred to it.

The fourth prince, Ernest Augustus, Duke of Cumberland, was, by all accounts, a fearsome individual, fully capable, it was said, of murdering the infant Victoria, his niece, who stood between him and the British crown. He had, it was rumoured, murdered his own valet in a fit of rage: his wife, Frederica of Mecklenburg-Strelitz, had a similar reputation—one of her two former husbands had died 'too conveniently'. But whatever the real story behind these alleged crimes and wicked intents, nothing could be proved.

Nor were the rumours ever substantiated that the Duke practised incest with his sister Sophia, though in 1829 one Captain Garth was said to be their son,* and it was rumoured that the royal family (apart from George III, who was not let

* See page 163.

Dorothy Jordan, the actress mistress of the future King William IV. Her earnings from the stage supplemented her lover's income.

Queen Victoria with her Highland servant, John Brown, falsely reputed as her lover after the death of the Prince Consort.

(Above left) Lillie Langtry, 'the Jersey lily'—one of the greatest beauties of Victorian England and mistress of the future Edward VII.

(Above right) Daisy Brooke, Countess of Warwick, the society belle who lost the affections of the Prince of Wales (the future King Edward VII) when she tried to convert him to Socialism.

Alice Keppel, Edward VII's last love.

into the secret) were at their wits' end to keep the scandal from breaking. In fact, gossips whispered terrible things about Cumberland and his sister, about Cumberland and the infinite variety of sexual perversions which he practised in his mirror-lined bedroom at St James's. No one was therefore surprised when Lady Lyndhurst, wife of the Lord Chancellor, alleged that the Duke had attempted to rape her in her drawing-room, and when Lord Graves cut his own throat after hearing rumours that Cumberland had seduced his wife.

Cumberland was certainly regarded as an ogre and a monster in his day, whatever the truth of the stories about him, and no one was sorry when, in 1837, he went off to reign in Hanover (the duchy had become a kingdom in 1814, but it was governed by the Salic Law which forbade inheritance by a woman, so when Victoria succeeded her Uncle William on the British throne, Ernest Augustus took Hanover as a consolation prize). He died fourteen years later.

The Duke of Sussex was more like Clarence and Kent than Cumberland. He, Augustus, actually made a career of matrimony, though not of the sort blessed by the Royal Marriage Act. Asthmatic and valetudinarian, he enjoyed annual holidays in the sun for his health, and while in Rome, in 1793, he met and fell in love with a woman some years his senior, Lady Augusta Murray. They married secretly and had already produced a son, Augustus d'Este, when, in the summer of 1794, an ecclesiastical Court was convened to discover the truth behind rumours that the Duke had contravened the Royal Marriage Act, and promptly declared the union invalid. Nevertheless, Augustus and Augusta were not daunted by the ruling but continued to live together abroad and in England, adding a daughter to their family in 1801.

But then, some ten years after the wedding, the couple parted—whether through the infidelity of either party, or because the Prince needed Parliament's approval of his life-style to gain a grant of money, it is impossible now to trace. Certainly, a few years later, Augustus and his wife were on bad terms, with him initiating one court action against her to prevent her using the style of Duchess and another to deprive her of custody of their children. Nevertheless, he was never so certain of the illegality of their marriage as to marry again while Lady Augusta lived, and it was not until May 1831, a year after her death, that Sussex once again broke the law, now marrying the widow Lady Cecilia Buggin, née Underwood. Apparently she proved more congenial to him than her predecessor, for they continued together until parted by death: in 1840 Queen Victoria, who could not officially recognise the marriage, created Lady Buggin Duchess of Inverness to please her Uncle Augustus, so that there was the absurdity at public functions of the couple's introduction as "His Royal Highness the Duke of Sussex and Her Grace the Duchess of Inverness", a bewilderment to the uninformed.

The last of the sons of George III who survived to maturity was the unexceptionable, unobtrusive Adolphus, Duke of Cambridge. He lived quietly and usefully at Hanover during his brothers' reigns, devoted to his German wife Augusta of Hesse-Cassel and to the three children whom they produced in (vain) hopes of their one day inheriting the crown. However, the Hanoverian strain of wildness which passed him by appeared in his son, to the horror of that George Cambridge's cousin, Queen Victoria.

There are, of course, six royal sisters to take into account when considering the sexuality of George III's children. Only the eldest was married according to the manner of the usual run of princesses, but even then, she was in her mid-twenties when she went to the altar, considerably older than was the norm for royal brides. The younger princesses were kept at home, as companions to their mother, under conventual rule.

Ever since the Middle Ages, and the courtly love convention, married women of the aristocracy had been recipients of illicit love-making, but their virgin sisters were straitly guarded for fear of their losing a good match by gaining a reputation for promiscuity: any princess sullied by scandal would lose her prime asset, her marriageability.

The daughters of George III and Charlotte of Mecklenburg-Strelitz should have been married young as were most of their caste: they were, like their brothers, too highly sexed to be allowed to live unwed. Not, of course that they were encouraged to fill the void with lovers: when they did so it was secretly—only the results gave them away to their sorrowing parents.

For nearly thirty years, the second daughter, Princess Augusta, loved and yearned for marriage with Major-General Sir Brent Spencer. He came (inevitably, for the princesses had few contacts outside the home circle) from the royal household: he was one of the King's equerries when the couple first met, in about the year 1800, when Augusta was already in her thirties. Then, for years, Spencer was away on active service in the army, with the Princess daily praying for his preservation from French shot and shell. She never dared beg her father's blessing to their marriage but, during George III's illness in 1811, she did approach her brother George, then Regent, for his help in arranging the match. No evidence as to the outcome remains: Spencer was certainly well received at Court in the years that followed, but that is all that can be known. Whether Augusta married him privately with or without her family's approval, or whether she was so secretly his mistress that her mother never suspected, remains a mystery.

Even more mysterious is the illness of the sixteen-year-old Princess Elizabeth in 1787: it was rumoured that she was then pregnant, having married (of course, illegally) one of the royal pages, by whom she had a daughter. Certainly, Elizabeth always longed for conventional marriage, eagerly seizing upon the prospect of any potential bridegroom who came her way, but subject to parental approval, which was not forthcoming, she remained 'on the shelf' until the age of forty-seven, when at last the suit of a German, the Hereditary Prince of Hesse-Homburg, was found acceptable by her possessive mother, Queen Charlotte.

Princess Sophia did give birth to an illegitimate child: of that, at least, there can be no doubt. When she was twenty-two, she had a son, not by her brother Cumberland as was alleged but by General Thomas Garth, thirty-three years her senior. Like Spencer, Garth was a royal equerry and a military commander, and one of the few men received on an intimate footing in the royal family. However, none of the circumstances of the liaison are known, beyond the fact that the family did their utmost to shield Sophia from shame, and that they did not cast off Garth, as one might expect. (This has even been explained by the suggestion that he was not, after all, the Princess's lover but took that credit to obscure her even more heinous relations with Cumberland.)

The fourth transgressor was Princess Amelia, whose tastes closely corresponded with those of her sisters: she loved General the Honourable Sir Charles Fitzroy (a descendant of one of Charles II's bastards), yet another equerry, soldier and middle-aged Romeo. Amelia's letters to Fitzroy prove her love for him: there is, however, no evidence that she was ever his mistress, or that they were married, despite the Princess's repeated assertions that she considered herself Fitzroy's wife. Amelia died in November 1810, of tuberculosis, leaving her few possessions to her "beloved Charles".

The lives and loves of King George IV and his brothers and sisters provide a good argument for the case in favour of early, arranged marriages. Had each been wed, at the age of fifteen, to equally innocent partners, the force of their sexuality might have been channelled, like their parents', into matrimonial fidelity. The Dukes of Clarence, Kent, Sussex and Cambridge proved themselves adept in domestic life, not prone, like their brothers George of Wales, Frederick of York and Ernest Augustus of Cumberland, to polygamy: had they been given their chance, as young men, of marital stability, they might have proved imitators of their virtuous father. Had the Princesses been given the chance of independence and motherhood at the natural age, they might have needed no other outlet for their over-flowing passions.

But history is full of 'might have beens'.

13

Bertie

Henry I, with his twenty-odd bastards; Edward IV, "licentious in the extreme"; Charles II, 'the merry monarch'; George IV, 'the prince of pleasure': every now and then the royal family has produced a man of immense sexual appetites. The most recent, perhaps the most promiscuous of them all, was Edward VII, who brought into the twentieth century a final, exuberant defiance of sexual virtue before respectability engulfed the royal family.

It is always remarked, in any study of the life of Albert Edward, Prince of Wales (later King Edward VII), that his wayward passions ill-accorded with the unblemished fidelity and mutual devotion of his parents, Victoria and Albert. And yet, 'Bertie' was not only the nephew of the English satyrs George IV and Frederick, Duke of York, but grandson and nephew of Ernest I and Ernest II, Dukes of Saxe-Coburg-Gotha, "fathers of their people" in more than one sense. Where Victoria saw her paternal uncles in the person of her son, Albert recognised the traits of his father and brother. However, where Albert was too pure himself to have any insight into Bertie's fall, Victoria may have understood the Prince's temptations only too well: she always said that her son was "a caricature" of herself.

Queen Victoria is generally associated with the extremes of prudery and strict morality to which her middle-class subjects adhered, but, where the pattern of Victorian wives merely suffered their husbands' advances and were proud to say that no man had ever seen them naked, Victoria was among the most passionate and demanding of women, loving her Albert as intensely in their physical partnership as in their emotional relations. "What a dreadful going to bed," the Queen later recorded after the Prince Consort's death, "What a contrast to that tender lover's love. All alone!"[1]

There would have been a national outcry had Victoria ever

sought to compensate herself for her loss by taking lovers: in fact, she would never have contemplated such a prospect. Consciously, she would have been revolted by the idea, with her high principles and firm religious faith; but, more powerfully perhaps, there was an instinctive revulsion which, had strong temptation ever presented itself, would surely have held her back. As a child, she had seen her own widowed mother in the embrace of Sir John Conroy, their household comptroller at Kensington Palace. Almost certainly Victoria never suspected any worse than the kiss or caress which she witnessed, but at once Conroy became, to her, a monster. The power which he wielded over her mother, the Duchess of Kent, was the bane of her young life: for years Conroy attempted to gain an ascendancy over Victoria herself, to rule through her when she should come to the throne. As Queen, however, Victoria was vicious in her rejection of her weak mother and adamant in her enmity to Conroy. Even Albert, for much of their marriage, was not accorded such power as Conroy had sought: Victoria was always jealous of the rights of her independence as queen, if not as wife.

No man could replace Albert in her love after his death; no man would be allowed to rule her by blandishments and flattery as Conroy had ruled Victoire of Kent. The Queen accepted the sentimentalised devotion of her Prime Minister Disraeli in the same way as, in her teens, she had accepted the paternal solicitude of her Prime Minister Melbourne: but then, neither was a threat to her integrity. At the same time, Victoria accepted the rough devotion of her Highland servant, John Brown, allowing him the familiarities of a rather wayward lap-dog: but then the attentions of one of his lowly rank could never, she believed, be misunderstood—in fact, those who had most denigrated her retirement into seclusion with her grief at Albert's death, now came forward to slander her as 'Mrs Brown', with no justification. Nevertheless, it is Victoria the 'one-man woman' who has passed into popular legend.

It seems possible that the Queen was amazed at her own enjoyment of physical passions in her marriage, seeing in herself a true daughter of the Hanoverians, and that she recognised in her son's promiscuity what she might have been had Albert not come soon enough to 'save her from herself'. The anomaly of her severity and sympathy for her son would be hard to understand without such a background.

Victoria and Albert put more care into, and took more interest in, the upbringing of their children than most royal parents of their time. At Windsor and Buckingham Palace, the children spent most of their day in the charge of governesses and tutors, but on holiday at Osborne and Balmoral they were their parents' constant companions. And yet, for all this enlightened approach, the Queen and her consort made serious, tragic mistakes in their dealings with their eldest son, which contributed to his undoing of their careful tutelage.

Bertie grew up under the shadow of his brilliant, articulate and energetic elder sister, Victoria, Princess Royal. He was forever being compared unfavourably with her: a sure deterrent, as educational psychologists would note, against his uninhibited development. Prince Albert could have forgiven his son for having only average intelligence, but he could not forgive his lack of diligence, application to study and submission to duty. Albert had that sort of 'over-grown' conscience which drives a man to an early grave: he over-worked and over-worried; he took on more responsibility than his frail body could bear. When, in 1861, he succumbed to typhoid (or maybe to cancer, as has recently been suggested), even Victoria recognised that he had not the will to live, to go on toiling as he had over the past twenty years. Such a man could not understand the weaknesses of his eldest son, who could be shamed into promising self-reform but who had not the same inner drive for perfection as his father.

Victoria and Albert admitted to themselves their failure with Bertie, though Albert at least never, to the end of his life, lowered the absurdly high standards which he demanded of the young Prince of Wales. When it was revealed to Albert, by a 'concerned' friend, in 1861, that Bertie had lost his virginity in the bed of a young actress, the Prince Consort was appalled.

Like Victoria, Albert had more than objective reasons to loathe promiscuity. His own father, himself a roué, had cast off his wife for her adultery, leaving Albert (four years old at the time of his parents' separation) with a horror of extra-marital love.

Already ill, the Prince Consort sped to Cambridge to confront his son with his sin. Bertie was as contrite and penitent as his father could wish, but the whole affair had dealt a hard blow to Albert's constitution. Since the furore over the young Prince's 'fall', as his parents termed it, occurred only weeks before Albert's death, Victoria long blamed her son for worrying her husband into his grave: "Oh! that boy," she wrote, "much as I pity, I never can or shall look at him without a shudder. . . ."[2]

Bertie's case casts strong doubt on the theory that an early marriage can prevent a career of promiscuity. The Prince was wed, in March 1863 (at the age of twenty-two), to Princess Alexandra of Denmark, as "bonnie and blithe and good and gay" a young woman as his mother could find, but though he was charmed with her, he was even more charmed to taste the freedom of his new position. The Queen still tried to exercise restraint on her son's behaviour, but gradually he slipped from her grasp. And, while Victoria remained in the deepest seclusion, mourning her Albert, not even attempting to keep the figurehead of monarchy before her people, the Prince of Wales took over her leadership of society—with all its temptations.

The Queen had never cared greatly for her aristocracy. Albert had taught her to prize the simplicity of the family circle and the delights of home-made entertainment, and the grandeur and luxury, the extravagance and loose-living of the nobility had appalled him—and thus Victoria also. Their eldest son, on the other hand, found his true métier in the society of the 'idle rich'.

The Princess Alexandra was really as home-loving as her mother-in-law, but, as Bertie dragged her into the social round, the Queen unfairly blamed the girl for allowing the Prince to fritter away his time, his money and his talents. Bertie loved Alexandra, but it was no *grande passion*; certainly she loved him, but as the years passed, she found more satisfaction in motherhood. The Prince's innumerable infidelities sorely grieved her, and more than once her protracted visit to her homeland was a reproach for his unkindness. But Alexandra was bred to such a life: she was by no means the only princess in Europe who had to wear a brave face and stiffen her back, to ignore the sniggers of her companions when yet another *petite amie* was presented to her Court by her husband.

Partly, Bertie's amorous career owed its fame to the fact that he had no formal career. Until, in his sixties, he succeeded to the throne, he was accorded no active role in government. His mother firmly refused to share her power, or to train the Prince for his future responsibilities. She, having come to the throne at the age of eighteen, had learned her craft under the tutelage of her Uncle Leopold,* of Lord Melbourne and Prince Albert; obtusely, she never realised that her son, even in middle age, might be fit for her work before he wore her crown, while at the same time deploring his idleness.

Thus, Bertie's year had less to do with the terms of Parliament than with the sporting calendar. In the autumn he went shooting on his estate in Norfolk, or on the moors of his friends; in the winter he enjoyed the pleasures of the London season; in the spring he visited Biarritz; in the summer he was to be found at a German spa, usually Homburg or, latterly, Marienbad. In England there were ladies of fashion to keep him from boredom (his perpetual fear), or an invigorating excursion into low-life to be relished; abroad, there were the professional *cocottes* who made their fortunes from catering for the bizarre tastes of rich men, who could not expect their wives to demean themselves to sexual experiment—at least, not for their husbands' pleasure.

Had Britain boasted a 'purple Press' in the nineteenth century, it would have suffered no shortage of copy. Society ladies—married, of course—had their lovers; their lords might prefer to find amusement in the high-class brothels which abounded in the West End of London. These people were the Prince's chosen friends.

At home, Bertie's preference was for mature, sophisticated women with blind or complaisant husbands: he was always fearful of scandal, though that did nothing to interfere with his sport. Yet twice he was brought to the brink of disaster. First, in 1868, he was subpoenaed as a witness in the Mordaunt divorce case, and asked, in open court, to declare if there had been any "improper familiarity" or "criminal act" between himself and the frail beauty Harriet Mordaunt. There had not, the Prince firmly averred (though the terms of the question allowed latitude for an elastic conscience). Surprisingly, Queen Victoria rallied to her son's defence, giving him as much sympathy and support as did Princess Alexandra, who appeared with her husband in theatres and at balls to give the lie to the gossips' rumours that she believed in his adultery. So low was Bertie's stock in the country after this incident that it was generally feared that he would be forced to abdicate should his mother die in the near future.

---

* Leopold of Saxe-Coburg-Saalfeld, formerly the husband of George IV's daughter Charlotte; he became King of the Belgians in 1831.

Then, in 1871, he was struck by typhoid, exactly ten years to the very month after his father's fatal illness. The whole nation waited with baited breath for the fever's crisis to come: then, the telegraphs flashed the news that the Prince of Wales was out of danger. Princess Alexandra nursed him back to health. All was well between them.

Had the Aylesford divorce case, of 1876, come to the courts, however, Bertie's reputation might never have recovered.

One of the Prince's cronies, 'Sporting Joe' Aylesford, had a beautiful wife, Edith, who was the mistress of Lord Blandford. In February 1876, she wrote to her husband, in India (which he was touring in the entourage of the Prince of Wales), requesting a divorce to enable her to marry her lover. When it was represented to her that she and her future husband would be outcasts from society (divorce was still a disgrace, even in the 'fastest' set, Edith Aylesford tried to recant—but now her husband would not let her. Blandford's brother, Lord Randolph Churchill, put pressure on Bertie to have Aylesford change his mind, and, when the Prince refused, threatened to produce Bertie's own letters to Lady Aylesford, though his liaison with her had ended several years previously; Churchill also went to Princess Alexandra with the story, warning her that he would reveal all if her husband did not prevent Aylesford's petitioning for divorce. Again subordinating her chagrin to the Prince's best interests, the Princess went to meet him at the Isle of Wight, on his return from the East, and together they brazened out the scandal. The loyal Aylesford postponed his divorce for some five years, by which time the Prince's involvement had been, if not forgotten, at least put into perspective.

For the most part, Bertie's *affaires* were condoned by society, and the ladies whom he honoured went under the polite fiction of being his 'friends'. But a shrewd hostess knew exactly whom to invite to share her table when the Prince was her guest—and whose husband should not be included in the party. From the 1870s until his death in 1910, Bertie was always keeping one long-term mistress (though none of them would aspire to the title of *maîtresse-en-titre*, such was their discretion) and still found the energy to take on the occasional chorus-girl.

The most fascinating of his mistresses was 'the Jersey Lily', Mrs Edward Langtry, née Emilie Charlotte ('Lillie') le Breton. Her great beauty had lifted her from obscurity on the fringe of the great world into the full glare of its centre. Awed silence fell when she entered a room in the full glory of a *grande toilette*; her photographs were on sale in every town in England; milliners and *couturiers* vied for her custom, allowing vast credit to see their creations carried into ballrooms and theatres by the reigning belle. Even Queen Victoria, usually careful of the sanctity of her portals, invited Lillie to her drawing-room; Princess Alexandra too fell under her spell.

Then, after some five years, the creditors and the bailiffs began to hover ever closer. But Lillie had more capital than mere money: having won plaudits in amateur theatricals, she became a professional actress and was an unqualified success. Her tour of the United States was a triumph, more from her reputation and associations than her acting ability. The Prince of Wales eased her path, but their *affaire* came amicably to an end. Lillie Langtry was as discreet as she was beautiful.

Frances, Lady Brooke (later Countess of Warwick) was less satisfactory. She had all the qualifications of a royal mistress (in fact, Queen Victoria had once deemed her worthy to be a royal bride; but 'Daisy' and Prince Leopold, the Queen's youngest son, both had other attachments; the Prince was best man at her wedding to Brooke in 1880): she was pretty, sophisticated, rich in her own right, blessed with a husband whose addiction to hunting, shooting and fishing took him away from home as often as she could wish. Unfortunately, by the time she came to Bertie, she had a 'past'. She had been the mistress of Lord Charles Beresford who had had the impudence to tire of her and return to his wife: when Daisy learned, in 1891, that Lady Charles was pregnant, she was furious. She wrote scathingly to her former lover, and her letter fell into the hands of his wife. Lady Charles threatened to use the document to ruin her rival, and the harassed Beresford sided with her. Only the firmest action by the Prince of Wales averted disaster.

He was infatuated with Daisy. And, at the same time, she provided him with some comfort when he desperately needed it, in the face of yet another scandal: this time not amorous but an affair of honour, when he had to appear in court to testify in a case of alleged cheating at cards by one of his friends. For once, Princess Alexandra was not tolerant of her husband's weakness: Bertie's real love for Daisy Brooke made her different from the usual run of his mistresses. Only the sudden death of their elder son, the Duke of Clarence, drew the royal couple together again.

The 1890s were the era of the greatest refinement of aristocratic society, with the nobility—not excluding the *nouveau riche*—bringing 'gracious living' to a fine art with their balls and parties, yachting and racing, expending for one day's pleasures sums that would keep a street of slum-dwellers in comfort for a year. Country-house parties were the rage, with dancing, sports, flirtation and practical jokes the order of the day. The Prince of Wales went from one great mansion to another, to be regaled with pretty women and rich foods (often prepared by Rosa Lewis, the Cockney cook who for a while served him in the bedroom as well as the kitchen). A scurrilous rhyme of Hilaire Belloc's of this period, detailing the 'naughty' pursuits of country-house visitors, had the revealing refrain, "And Mrs James will entertain the King". There was always a 'Mrs James' of some complexion willing to open her bedroom door to her future soveregn in his nocturnal wanderings.

The nineties were the decade of the Countess of Warwick, until she 'got religion' and devoted her considerable talents to worthier causes than the Prince's pleasure. In 1894 she had given a sumptuous ball at Warwick Castle, which a Socialist journalist had denounced as criminal, in the face of the dreadful poverty of the working class. His polemic had brought her up with a start: soon she was crusading for the poor on her own account, pestering the Prince to subscribe to her pet schemes and charities. Her political involvements became acutely embarrassing to him. Still, her new interests prevented her being too disconsolate when she was replaced.

Occasionally, the Prince's English mistresses would accompany him on his foreign holidays (the Princess withdrew happily to Denmark, or to visit her sister the Tsarina of Russia); more often, he went *en garçon*, in a noisy crowd of male friends. In Paris, his reputation was formidable: many a woman who had received no more notice than a *coup d'œil* from the *Prince de Galles* boasted of her conquest, but there were many others who had more tangible proof of his interest.

Paris of the *belle epoque* has been immortalised by Toulouse-Lautrec's flamboyant paintings: like Bertie he was a frequenter of the Moulin Rouge, where they both appreciated the Cockney-like vulgarity of La Goulue, the CanCan dancer, who had no compunction in commanding her royal admirer, in the most raucous tones, to order champagne for everyone in the house. Then there was the sylph-like Cora Pearl, who is reputed once to have feasted her friends, the Prince included, but did not join them at table until, at the end of the banquet, she leaped stark naked from under a mammoth dish-cover. And there was the great Sarah Bernhardt, the *tragedienne*, a celebrity in her own right, who did not need royal associations to crown her own eminence, and who could certainly not be counted among the notorious courtesans (known as *les horizontales*) who made an art of and a fortune from their ancient profession. In brilliantly lit restaurants and discreetly darkened rooms, the Prince of Wales disported himself free of the restraints of his home and ever-watchful mother.

His escapades might have been worse. In Bavaria only half a century earlier, 'mad King Ludwig' had fallen prey to the rapacious Lola Montez, a nymphomaniac of amazing stamina, almost provoking revolution for his follies; in Austria, Crown Prince Rudolf and his teenaged mistress Maria Vetsera were found dead together in bed—shot, according to Rudolf's last note, by himself in the desperation of love. Almost every monarch, every prince, every duke, archduke and grand duke in Europe had his mistress from nobility or chorus-line, or at least the *entrée* to the gold and glass brothels of the capitals— with or without attendant scandals. Indeed, could recently raised suspicions be proved that Bertie's own son 'Eddy', Duke of Clarence, was the infamous 'Jack the Ripper', murderer of East End prostitutes, the Prince of Wales's own proclivities would be innocuous in comparison.

As it was, he came to reign, in 1901, with a high reputation as a connoisseur of women and his subjects' low expectations of his ability to rule. King Edward VII surprised them all. He took remarkably well to his duties and, if he had little interest in party politics and home policies, he had an acute understanding of international diplomacy. Related as he was to most of the crowned heads of Europe—the German Kaiser was his nephew, the Russian Tsar his wife's—he was well placed to take a broad and long-term view of Continental alignments. One fruit of his 'mis-spent' years in France was his *Entente Cordiale*, which ensured Britain a loyal ally across the Channel in the dark days of 1914.

In the last years of the nineteenth century, Bertie had found his perfect match in a young, buxom, quiet woman, Mrs Alice Keppel, who was the epitome of a mistress's virtues. She made no demands on the King's purse or on the time which he must now devote to business; she was there when she was wanted, in the background when her presence might be embarrassing; she could be relied on to keep the King from boredom and to moderate his greed for the rich food and drink which were ruining his health. Her partner in this enterprise was Miss Agnes Keyser, one of the few unmarried women who attracted Bertie, though it is unlikely that she, a staid, prim nurse, was his mistress: in her homely rooms in her private hospital, she soothed his restless, tired brain and body and plied him with nourishing plain food which he, childlike, dared not refuse.

When King Edward lay dying, in 1910, Queen Alexandra had the generosity to call Mrs Keppel to his bedside. Alice had always behaved with the utmost respect and tact towards the Queen (unlike many other women who had been in her position), and she was rewarded with respect and kindness in return.

Just as 1914 marked the end of an era for the nation, with the coming of world war and the changes it wrought in social and political life, so the death of King Edward VII in 1910 brought to a close the long ages of the British kings and queens who sought love and sexual fulfilment outside marriage. The new king, George V, and his queen, Mary of Teck, were a latter-day George III and Charlotte, their dignity in public matched by their propriety at home. Around them thrones tumbled, through war and revolution, but they were secure in the love of their subjects.

Had George's elder brother Eddy, the late Duke of Clarence, lived to succeed their father on the throne, the situation might have been different. Mary of Teck had been his fiancée in the last weeks of his life, brought forward by Queen Victoria to tame and reform the wayward, unpleasant young man, but even she could not have worked miracles. Britain and her Empire were safer in the hands of the dutiful, good-natured George who succeeded Eddy as their father's heir and Mary's fiancé.

No more potent proof that the age of the royal paramour was over could be found than the abdication crisis of 1936, when the son of George and Mary, King Edward VIII, gave up his throne rather than bring his crown, Church and family into disrepute by marrying a divorcée. As Governor of the Church of England (legacy of Henry VIII's desire for Anne Boleyn), Edward VIII could not marry a divorcée: the Anglican hierarchy forbade such marriages, even where the innocent party in a divorce was involved.

Other kings, throughout Europe, had taken 'morganatic' wives—women whose rank or status barred them from sharing a throne, who were content with a private, though legal, marriage, and whose children would not be allowed to inherit the crown. Such marriages, however, have never been customary in Britain.

Time and again the American divorcée Mrs Simpson offered to disappear from Edward VIII's life, to release him from the intolerable dilemma in which his royalty and her past placed them. It took much heart-searching for the King to make his decision: he knew his duty to his kingdom and empire, but he could not face a lifetime on the throne without Mrs Simpson beside him. On 11 December 1936 he penned his signature to the deed of abdication, and that night spoke to his subjects over the radio. He told them what he had done, adding, "... you must believe me when I tell you that I have found it impossible to carry the heavy burden of responsibility and discharge my duties as king as I would wish to do, without the help and support of the woman I love'.

A lesser man, a less scrupulous woman, in a less self-conscious era, would have suffered no such crisis of conscience. But for this man and this woman, in the twentieth century, illicit love, such as so many previous monarchs had enjoyed without qualms, was unthinkable. Yet, where monarchs and mistresses had once gone their way without heed for public opinion and Christian ethics, husband and wife now suffered for their integrity and proud morality amid public censure of their marriage.

The sexual transgressions of past monarchs were known in their times through gossip, or brought to light in later years in published diaries and memoirs of courtiers. Today, the lives of members of the royal family are open books, through the avid interest of the media: a prince or princess has only to appear in public with a certain companion more than once for romantic speculations to be aroused. And, while Press spies are to be found outside the bedroom doors of pop-stars and politicians, actors and artists, footballers and financiers, those of the royal family are surveyed with scarcely more respectful restraint.

But the lives of modern royal personages find far more coverage in the cosy columns of women's magazines than in the scandal-sheets. Standards have changed: in the past royal *amours* could be viewed with tolerance, even used as an excuse for the sins of lesser mortals; today, more is expected of the royal family, higher standards of morality are demanded from them than are applied to any other section of the population.

Only future years can tell if a King George VII, a Henry IX or a Mary III will provide the British people with yet more stories of royal paramours.

Sources of Quotations

CHAPTER 1

1 *The great rolls of the pipe of the reign of Henry II, fifth to thirty-fourth years* (Pipe Roll Society, 1884–1925), thirtieth year, pp. 134–5
2 *Documents illustrative of English history of the thirteenth and fourteenth centuries*, ed. H. Cole (1844) p. 267
3 Giraldus Cambrensis (Gerald of Wales), *Opera*, volume IV, ed. J. S. Brewer (Rolls Series, no. 21, 1861–91), p. 368
4 *Polychronicon Ranulphi Higden*, ed. J. R. Lumby (Rolls Series, 1865–86), volume VIII, p. 55

CHAPTER 2

1 William of Malmesbury, *Gesta regum Anglorum*, ed. W. Stubbs (1887)
2 C. Marlowe, *The troublesome reign and lamentable death of Edward II, King of England* (1594), lines 688–98
3 *Vita Edwardi secundi*, ed. N. Denholm Young (Nelson, 1957), p. 143

CHAPTER 3

1 A. Strickland, *Lives of the Queens of England* (1855), volume I, p. 589
2 William Langland, *Piers Plowman*, Passus II
3 Geoffrey Chaucer, *The Canterbury Tales*, trs. N. Coghill (Penguin Books, 1951), pp. 104–5
4 *Froissart's Chronicle*, trs. Lord Berners, ed. W. Paton Ker (David Nutt: Tudor Translations, 1901–3), volume VI, p. 191
5 *Vita et gesta Henrici quinti*, ed. T. Hearne (1727), p. 13
6 D. Mancini, *The Usurpation of Richard III*, trs. C. A. J. Armstrong (Clarendon Press, 1969), p. 67
7 T. More, *The History of King Richard III*, ed. R. S. Sylvester (Complete works, Yale edition, II, 1963), p. 64
8 *Ibid.*, p. 62

9 Ibid., p. 57
10 Ibid., p. 44
11 Ibid., p. 56
12 *Unfortunate Royal Mistresses* (1825), pp. 75–6
13 P. Lindsay, *King Richard III* (Ivor Nicholson & Watson, 1933), pp. 237–8

CHAPTER 4

1 *Calendar of letters, despatches and state papers . . . Spain*, ed. G. A. Bergenroth *et al.* (1862–96), volume I, pp. 36–41
2 *Ibid.*
3 J. Stow, *Chronicle* (1615 edition), p. 526
4 *The Love-letters of Henry VIII*, ed. H. Savage (Allan Wingate, 1949), pp. 33–4
5 C. A. Wriothesley, *A Chronicle of England*, ed. W. D. Hamilton (Camden Society, new series, 1875), volume I, p. 36
6 *Letters and papers, foreign and domestic, of the reign of Henry VIII*, ed. J. S. Brewer *et al.* (1862–1932), volume X, p. 243
7 G. Burnet, *The History of the Reformation of the Church of England*, ed. E. Nares (1839), volume IV, p. 505

CHAPTER 5

1 A. Strickland, *op. cit.*, volume IV, pp. 42–3
2 *Calendar of State Papers . . . in the Archives of Simancas*, ed. M. A. S. Hume (1892), pp. 57–8
3 Ibid., p. 387
4 A. Strickland, *op. cit.*, volume IV, pp. 312–3

CHAPTER 6

1 J. Harington, *Nugae Antiquae* (1804 edition), volume I, pp. 390–7
2 *Letters of the kings of England*, ed. J. O. Halliwell (1846), · volume II, pp. 126–33
3 H. Wotton, *Reliquae Wottonianiae* (1654), p. 21
4 *Letters . . .* , *op. cit.*, volume II, p. 156
5 Ibid., pp. 232–6
6 A. Weldon, *The Court and Character of James I* (1650) in *The Secret History of the Court of James I*, ed. W. Scott (1811), volume II, pp. 1–5
7 S. R. Gardiner, *History of England from the Accession of James I to the Outbreak of the Civil War* (1883–4), volume VI, p. 123

CHAPTER 7

1 Samuel Pepys, *Diary*, 31 December 1662
2 John Evelyn, *Diary*, 8 August 1649 and 15 July 1685
3 Edward Hyde, Earl of Clarendon, *Continuation of the Life of* . . . *Clarendon* (1828), paragraph 392
4 C. H. Hartmann, *The King my Brother* (Heinemann, 1954), p. 201
5 J. Evelyn, *op. cit.*, 8 February 1685

CHAPTER 8

1 G. Roberts, *The Life, Progresses and Rebellion of James, Duke of Monmouth* (1844), volume I, p. 154
2 S. Pepys, *op. cit.*, 13 October 1665

CHAPTER 9

1 James II, *Papers of devotion*, ed. G. Davies (Roxburghe Club, 1925), p. 17
2 *Letters of two queens*, ed. B. Bathurst (Robert Holden, 1924), pp. 60–61
3 G. Burnet, *History of his own time* (1838), p. 439
4 *Letters of two queens, op. cit.*, p. 91
5 G. J. Renier, *William of Orange* (P. Davies, 1932), pp. 68–9
6 Sarah Churchill, Duchess of Marlborough, *Account of the conduct of the Dowager Duchess of Marlborough* . . ., ed. N. Hooker (1742), pp. 75–6
7 *Ibid.*, p. 14
8 Blenheim MSS G–1–9
9 J. Swift, *Prose works*, ed. H. Davis (Blackwell, 1953), volume VIII, p. 153
10 G. Burnet, *op. cit.* (1823 edition), volume VI, pp. 32–3
11 Sarah Churchill, *op. cit.*, p. 183
12 *Ibid.*, p. 184
13 W. S. Churchill, *Marlborough: His Life and Times* (Harrap, 1947), volume II, pp. 640–1
14 Blenheim MSS. E 17

CHAPTER 10

1 H. Walpole, *Reminiscences*, ed. E. Paget Toynbee (Clarendon Press, 1924), pp. 29–30

2 W. H. Wilkins, *The Love of an Uncrowned Queen* (1900), p. 153
3 Lord Hervey, *Some materials towards a history of the reign of George II*, ed. R. Sedgwick (Eyre & Spottiswoode, 1931), volume I, p. 11
4 *Ibid.*, volume I, p. 93
5 *Letters of . . . the Earl of Chesterfield*, ed. Lord Mahon (1892), volume II, p. 459
6 Lord Hervey, *op. cit.*, volume I, p. 67
7 *Ibid.*, volume I, p. 69
8 British Museum Additional Manuscripts 22627 f. 7
9 Lord Hervey, *op. cit.*, volume II, p. 748

CHAPTER 11

1 *The correspondence of George, Prince of Wales, 1770–1812*, ed. A. Aspinall (Cassell, 1963–71), volume IV, p. 48
2 *Ibid.*, volume III, p. 181
3 *Ibid.*, volume III, p. 194
4 *Ibid.*, volume III, p. 132

CHAPTER 12

1 M. Gillen, *The Prince and his Lady* (Sidgwick & Jackson, 1970), p. 214
2 T. Creevy, *Creevy Papers*, ed. H. Maxwell (John Murray, 1904), volume I, p. 269

CHAPTER 13

1 RA Vic. Add. MSS. Z261, the Royal Library, Windsor Castle. Copyright reserved
2 *Dearest Mama*, ed. R. Fulford (Evans Brothers, 1968), p. 30

Further Reading

Some three hundred works were consulted during the preparation of this book: from medieval chronicles to the most recent biographies. Most of these books are not easily available to the general reader, and the list given below is for further reading rather than a full bibliography, and comprises mainly those books which are either in print or accessible in public libraries.

CHAPTER 1

There are many excellent biographies of the early medieval kings, very few of their queens, none in recent years of the royal mistresses.

Standard works on the kings include: D. C. Douglas, *William the Conqueror* (Eyre & Spottiswoode, 1964); J. T. Appleby, *Henry II* (Bell, 1965); W. L. Warren, *King John* (Eyre & Spottiswoode, 1962); F. M. Powicke, *King Henry III and the Lord Edward* (Oxford University Press, 1947).

The eight-volume *Lives of the Queens of England* (1066 to 1714) by Agnes Strickland, first published in 1855, has been reprinted recently by Portway of Bath. Especially interesting are biographies of Eleanor of Aquitaine by R. Pernoud (Collins, 1967) and A. Kelly (Cassell, 1952).

CHAPTER 2

Among recent biographies of the kings mentioned in this chapter are: J. Gillingham, *Richard I* and C. Bingham, *Edward II* (both Weidenfeld & Nicolson, 1973); see also H. F. Hutchison, *Edward II: The Pliant King* (Eyre & Spottiswoode, 1971).

CHAPTER 3

Again there is a dearth of biographies of royal mistresses, but there is one recent and useful work on Alice Perrers: F. G. Kay, *Lady of the Sun* (Frederick Muller, 1966). Anya Seton's novel *Catherine* (Catherine Swynford, mistress then wife of John of Gaunt) gives a fascinating, detailed picture of Court life under Edward III and

Richard II (Hodder & Stoughton, 1954, and later editions; also paperback).

There is no recent biography of Jane Shore but she appears in Thomas More's history of the period: *Complete Works*, ed. R. S. Sylvester (Yale edition, volume II, 1963).

The kings: A. Steel, *Richard II* (Cambridge University Press, 1941); G. Mathew, *The Court of Richard II* (John Murray, 1968); C. Ross, *Edward IV* (Eyre Methuen, 1973); P. M. Kendall, *Richard III* (George Allen & Unwin, 1973).

The queens: J. J. Bagley, *Margaret of Anjou* (Herbert Jenkins, 1948); D. MacGibbon, *Elizabeth Woodville* (Arthur Barker, 1938).

CHAPTER 4

Of the many biographies of King Henry VIII, the best is that by J. J. Scarisbrick (Eyre & Spottiswoode, 1968), and a broader view of his personal life in N. Williams, *Henry VIII and his Court* (Weidenfeld & Nicolson, 1971). The King's sexuality is put well into perspective by comparison with that of King François I of France, *Prince of the Renaissance*, by D. Seward (Constable, 1973).

There is one work on Elizabeth Blount (by W. S. Childe-Pemberton, Eveleigh Nash, 1913), many on Anne Boleyn, of which the most useful are those by H. W. Chapman (Jonathan Cape, 1974) and M. L. Bruce (Collins, 1972). Biographies of Catherine of Aragon include works by F. Claremont (Robert Hale, 1939) and G. Mattingly (Jonathan Cape, 1942), and of Catherine Howard by L. B. Smith: *A Tudor tragedy* (Jonathan Cape, 1961).

CHAPTER 5

Dozens of books have been written on the life and reign of Elizabeth I. The most valuable modern works are the biographies by J. E. Neale (Jonathan Cape, 1934; frequently reprinted) and N. Williams (Weidenfeld & Nicolson, 1967), supplemented by the latter's *All the Queen's Men* (Weidenfeld & Nicolson, 1972).

The only recent biography of Robert Dudley is Elizabeth Jenkins' *Elizabeth and Leicester* (Gollancz, 1961). Works on the Queen's other favourites include: R. Lacey, *Robert, Earl of Essex: an Elizabethan Icarus* and *Sir Walter Ralegh* (Weidenfeld & Nicholson, 1971 and 1973 respectively); E. St J. Brookes, *Sir Christopher Hatton* (Jonathan Cape, 1946).

CHAPTER 6

The best recent biographies of James VI and I are those by D. Mathew (Eyre & Spottiswoode, 1967) and D. H. Willson (Jonathan

Cape, 1956; recently reprinted); G. P. V. Akrigg's *Jacobean Pageant* (Harvard University Press, 1962) provides a broader view of the reign.

There is no separate biography of Robert Carr, Earl of Somerset, but his career is traced in books on the Overbury murder: *Cast of Ravens* by V. White (John Murray, 1965) and *The Notorious Lady Essex* by E. le Comte (Robert Hale, 1969).

The most recent biographies of George Villiers, Duke of Buckingham are the short book by Hugh Ross Williamson (Duckworth, 1940) and L. Smith Gordon's translation of P. Erlanger's work (Hodder & Stoughton, 1953). A new full-scale biography is overdue and will be welcome when it does appear.

The life-story of Charles I is well told by C. Hibbert (Weidenfeld & Nicolson, 1968).

CHAPTER 7

Arthur Bryant's fine biography of Charles II (Collins, 1931) remains available in reprints, and may be supplemented by that by Maurice Ashley (Weidenfeld & Nicolson, 1971). H. W. Chapman's *Tragedy of Charles II* (Jonathan Cape, 1964) deals with his life before 1660.

An excellent biography of Barbara Villiers is Allen Andrews' *The Royal Whore* (Hutchinson, 1971). Bryan Bevan's book *James, Duke of Monmouth* (Robert Hale, 1973) draws on many earlier works for the life of the Duke's mother, Lucy Walter; by the same author are *Nell Gwyn* and *Charles II's French mistress—Louise de Keroualle* (Robert Hale, 1968 and 1970). The King's relations with his sister Henrietta Anne are examined in *Charles II and Madame*, by C. H. Hartmann, (Heinemann, 1934), who also collected their letters in *The King My Brother* (Heinemann, 1954); he also wrote the interesting *Vagabond Duchess—Hortense Mancini* (Routledge, 1926) and *La belle Stuart* (Routledge, 1924).

The Memoirs of Count Gramont, by Anthony Hamilton, edited by C. H. Hartmann and P. Quennell (Routledge, 1930)—and other, shorter editions—is a lively, scurrilous account of Court life after the Restoration, not always close to the truth but fascinating.

CHAPTER 8

The best recent biography of James, Duke of Monmouth is by Bryan Bevan (Robert Hale, 1973).

There has been no full-length biography of James II written in recent years, and that by F. C. Turner (Eyre & Spottiswoode, 1948) remains the standard work. The life of his wife, Mary of Modena, was written by C. Oman (Hodder & Stoughton, 1962) and Bryan Bevan (*I was James II's Queen*: Robert Hale, 1963). Bryan Bevan also wrote the most useful recent biography of *James III*—the Old

Pretender (Robert Hale, 1967). Of the many books on Charles Edward Stuart, *The Rash Adventurer* by M. Forster (Secker & Warburg, 1973) is the best of recent works. There is a biography of his wife, Louise of Stolberg, by M. Crosland (Oliver & Boyd, 1962).

CHAPTER 9

The lives of the joint sovereigns William and Mary have been re-examined by many historians recently. The best of their works are: *William and Mary*, by H. and B. van der Zee (Macmillan, 1973); N. A. Robb, *William of Orange* (Heinemann, 1966); *Mary II, Queen of England* by H. W. Chapman (Jonathan Cape, 1953; Cedric Chivers, Portway, 1972), and *William's Mary* by Elizabeth Hamilton (Hamish Hamilton, 1972).

Of the many biographies of Queen Anne, the best is by David Green (Collins, 1970), who also wrote the most comprehensive of recent works on Sarah Churchill, Duchess of Marlborough (Collins, 1967). In the same year appeared Iris Butler's *Rule of Three*, on Sarah, Anne and Abigail (Hodder & Stoughton).

CHAPTER 10

There is still no thorough study of the life of King George I, no book on Court life in his time which would fill out our sparse knowledge of his mistresses. However, interesting light is shed on the subject in the biographies of his mother, *Sophie, Electress of Hanover* by M. Kroll (Victor Gollancz, 1973) and his wife, *Sophie Dorothea* by R. Jordan (Constable, 1971).

Charles Chevenix Trench has supplied full details and analysis of the character and life of George II (Allen Lane, 1973), but the fascinating *Lady Suffolk and Her Circle*, by L. Melville, (Hutchinson, 1924) is now hard to find.

The most recent edition of Lord Hervey's memoirs—an invaluable source for the period—was published by William Kimber, 1952, almost the only reminiscences of the reign now generally available.

Poor Fred and the Butcher, by M. Marples (Michael Joseph, 1973) traces the careers of George II's sons the Prince of Wales and the Duke of Cumberland. 'Fred's' sons appear in *George III at Home* by N. Pain (Weidenfeld & Nicolson, 1974). An excellent biography of the unfortunate Caroline Matilda, Queen of Denmark, is that by H. W. Chapman (Jonathan Cape, 1971).

A fascinating work on French history of the time is *Madame de Pompadour* by Nancy Mitford (Hamish Hamilton, 1954; several times reprinted).

CHAPTER 11

By far the best life of George IV is that by Christopher Hibbert, in two parts: *George IV, Prince of Wales* (Longman, 1972) and *George IV, Regent and King* (Allen Lane, 1975). The most valuable book on Mrs Fitzherbert was written by Anita Leslie (Hutchinson, 1960).

The story of the unfortunate Caroline of Brunswick has been told several times, but *The Wanton Queen* by E. E. P. Tisdall (Stanley Paul, 1939) remains the best version.

CHAPTER 12

The most recent life of William (IV), Duke of Clarence is that by P. Ziegler (Collins, 1971) and of Mrs Jordan by B. Fothergill (Faber & Faber, 1965): her correspondence was edited by A. Aspinall in *Mrs Jordan and Her Family* (Arthur Barker, 1951).

There is a fine biography of Edward, Duke of Kent, by D. Duff (Stanley Paul, 1938; reprinted by Frederick Muller, 1973) and his relationship with Julie St Laurent is examined in *The Prince and His Lady*, by M. Gillen (Sidgwick & Jackson, 1970).

Two interesting lives of the Duke of Cumberland are those by Herbert van Thal (Arthur Barker, 1936) and G. M. Willis (Arthur Barker, 1954).

The lives of the brothers are dealt with collectively in *Royal Dukes* by R. Fulford (Collins, revised edition 1973) and of the princesses in *Six Royal Sisters* by M. Marples (Michael Joseph, 1969).

CHAPTER 13

The standard work on King Edward VII is the 'official' biography by Philip Magnus (John Murray, 1964); a lively account of his private life is J. Pearson's *Edward the Rake* (Weidenfeld & Nicolson, 1975).

On the King's mistresses, there is a biography of the Countess of Warwick by M. Blunden (Cassell, 1967) and of Lillie Langtry by J. Brough, *The Prince and the Lily* (Hodder & Stoughton, 1975).

Among much background material, some interesting works are: A. Leslie, *Edwardians in Love* (Hutchinson, 1972); V. Cowles, *Edward VII and His Circle* (Hamish Hamilton, 1956); J. Richardson, *The Courtesans* (Weidenfeld & Nicolson, 1967); Betty Kelen, *The Mistresses* (W. H. Allen, 1966); and R. Rudorff, *Belle Epoque* (Hamish Hamilton, 1972).

Speculations as to the sexual proclivities of Albert Victor, Duke of Clarence, are assessed in *Clarence* by M. Harrison (W. H. Allen, 1972).

Index